Praise for *Legally Savvy*

Zarinah Nadir has single handedly begun the dismantling of the mental barriers we all have concerning attorneys and the law. Her common sense explanations and down-to-earth approach are both disarming and extremely rare in this field. Zarinah's heart beats throughout this book making it a must read for anyone governed by the laws of this nation. This is a must have reference book for any diverse library and will serve as an educational tool for me and my business partners. Thank you, Zarinah Nadir; this is exactly what we all need!

> **– HAROLD G. BRANCH III,**
> *Globally Recognized Author, Speaker,*
> *Trainer & Founder of HomeBase Poetry*

I've spent my legal career focusing on making legal services accessible and affordable for everyone. *Legally Savvy* is a must read for anyone who believes in their rights to equal access to justice.

> **– KERI C. NORRIS,**
> *LegalShield Chief Legal Officer*

A paradigm shift! Zarinah gives a new perspective on how we should have ALWAYS been using and protecting our legal rights! Reading this book can help us all make pro-action our greatest reaction! It is an easy read and her personality shines through, making a seemingly confusing topic fun!

> **– JOSLYNN BROWN,**
> *Award-winning Entrepreneur & Entertainment*
> *Business Strategist, Young Pro Council Member*

Author Zarinah Nadir clearly explains why everyone, not just rich people and bad people, should utilize attorneys. The average, good, middle-class person should lawyer up often, and a cost/benefit analysis proves that it is worth it. Ms. Nadir does a wonderful job of helping Americans become exactly as the book's title says: "Legally Savvy."

– RONALD L. JONES, Attorney,
Partner at Davis Miles McGuire Gardner

Attorney Nadir expertly provides a road map for the unrepresented litigant to navigate the labyrinth of the modern legal system. Nadir identifies key areas that affect people's everyday lives and guides them on how to avoid legal problems before they occur! This book should be on everyone's book shelf!

– HOLLY MARSHALL, Attorney,
NAACP Litigators Award

Take the advice of the sister. Read *Legally Savvy* and become legally savvy. Knowing how the law works can help you build—and keep—wealth. It can help you avoid legal landmines or court battles. Hiring attorneys can save thousands of dollars. Attorneys can offer solutions and save deals, such as negotiating with a lender to allow a closing of a home sale to proceed. It is an important book, especially for immigrants and people working their way up who need to know and be able to use the legal system. Zarinah was profiled in my book as a girl willing to stand apart for her beliefs as a Muslim. She uses that serene strength as an attorney to help others.

– DONNA GEHRKE-WHITE,
Author of The Face Behind the Veil

Legally Savvy is a must read for everyone, young and old. Zarinah Nadir creatively brings legal challenges and fears to life, touching on a wide variety of topics with creative stories and representative data. She has created an informative book, with compelling insights and interesting examples that build foundational legal knowledge for the average every-day person. Knowledge is power and she has gifted her years of legal experience to her readers to help empower themselves to better navigate the world around them.

– **NANCY SPEIDEL,**
Founder and CEO,
iSAW International

As a Muslim woman who teaches financial literacy, I am delighted to know that Zarinah Nadir has shared with us valuable insider tips on how to incorporate being 'legally savvy' in our everyday lives. It is crucial for people (especially women of color) to understand the utmost importance of knowing your legal rights in the communities we live in. Preparation is essential to respond to unexpected circumstances. Our lives are ever changing and being keen on understanding how the legal system works in the United States gives the reader a sense of confidence and peace of mind that we can be proactive in securing our rights in society.

– **LISA HASHEM, Co-host**
'Muslim Women and Finance' Podcast

I have dealt with probably thousands of people over the years and Zarinah, by far, has been the most loving and pleasant person I've ever met. Always having kind words, it's almost hard to believe she's an attorney. Her heart is so big you feel as if you've known her for years. I'm excited for *Legally Savvy* as I know it will be real, genuine, and comes from a sincere place of wanting to help.

– TANISHA MORGAN,
Author of Memoirs of a Nail Tech,
Award winning Entrepreneur, World Traveler

Attorney Zarinah Nadir can be trusted as a billboard of hope. Without question, *Legally Savvy* is an atlas that provides peace of mind.

– DR. CORTEZ D. SIMS, Author,
Mental Health Coach

The vast majority of us, those who grew up without access to lawyers and knowledge of the legal system, owe Zarinah Nadir a world of thanks. *Legally Savvy* provides shortcuts and handy insights on how to work with the American legal system on your own. It provides the kind of basic guidance that can help you understand when you need a lawyer and, perhaps just as important, when you don't. If you aren't a lawyer or don't have one in the family, you should read *Legally Savvy* right away and recommend it to your friends.

– DEAN DOUGLAS SYLVESTER,
Former Dean and Research Professor of Arizona
State University College of Law

As an avid reader, I loved *Legally Savvy*! Zarinah Nadir is helping make equal justice a reality. Zarinah Nadir's *Legally Savvy* is an important tool in the mission for access to justice.

– JEFF BELL,
LegalShield CEO

One of the most powerful statements that Attorney Zarinah Nadir makes in *Legally Savvy* is "knowledge is power." *Legally Savvy* is an essential tool book providing foundational information to the learned and unlearned in the law. Attorney Nadir has written a book that must be read by all litigants, all lawyers, and all judges.

– JUDGE PENNY LADELL WILLRICH (RET.),
Maricopa County Superior Court

It is an honor and no false flattery that I esteem, Ms. Zarinah Nadir, Esq. author of the gift, *Legally Savvy*. Ms. Nadir is an extraordinary human being, a trail blazer, community influencer, and leader. She is a wise scholar respected by her peers, admired by her elders, and is inspiring future generations. Zarinah loves people and her passion shows up in her participation in assisting people to gain access to exercise their rights as an American and as a global citizen. I implore you to get a copy of this book, *Legally Savvy,* not only for yourself but for those you love. This book is a timely and needed gift to the "community where far too many Americans feel and often are denied their rights due to a lack of knowledge or lack of access to legal representation.

– KIANA MARIA STOREY-SEARS, MPA,
East Valley NAACP President,
Ebony Magazine National Shirley Chisholm Award Winner
& Governing Board Member of Mesa Public Schools

Legally
SAVVY

Published in the United States by Book Power Publishing, an imprint of Niyah Press, Detroit, Michigan.
www.bookpowerpublishing.com

Contact the author at: zarinah@belegallysavvy.com

First Edition
PRINTED IN THE UNITED STATES OF AMERICA.

ISBN: 978-1-945873-49-2

BOOK
POWER
PUBLISHING

Contents

FOR
WE,
THE
PEOPLE

Note To Reader

The information contained in this book does not constitute legal advice. It is intended as general information. Any reliance on the information herein is at your sole discretion. You are encouraged to speak with your attorney for understanding on how the law specifically applies to you. Additionally, you are encouraged to consult with your clergy on religious matters if you walk a particular spiritual path.

The stories shared here are for illustrative purposes only. Other than celebrities, the names and personally identifying characteristics have been changed. Any resemblance you see to yourself or someone you know is simply coincidental but a testament to how real life can get legal for more people than you think.

Foreword by Tracy Broughton, Ms. America 2011
ATTORNEY ZARINAH NADIR

YOUR GUIDE TO Avoiding Headaches and Heartbreaks IN *LOVE, LIFE,* AND *BUSINESS*

Legally SAVVY

"Powerful...A must-read for all"
- Judge Penny Ladell Willrich (Ret.), Maricopa County Superior Court

BOOK POWER PUBLISHING
Detroit, Michigan

Foreword

When I was asked to write the foreword to *Legally Savvy* I have to admit I was extremely honored and proud, and at the same time amazed that one simple idea can impact and change so many lives, as well as make a difference in the arena of social justice.

I met Zarinah when I was the keynote speaker for a *Ladies of Justice* event that our mutual friend Tanisha was hosting. Although she says she was enamored or "star struck" when we met, she doesn't know she touched me from the day that I met her. Zarinah left an impression, not of a stereotypical attorney, but of an amazing, powerful, loving, happy human being! Her character, kindness, positive energy, and passion to help others illuminated and was contagious. Any professional title she carried only complimented her other profound qualities and character.

Over the years, as I got to know her, a beautiful friendship and mutual appreciation ensued. I witnessed her incredible skill set in her craft and her leadership inside and outside of our company. I was inspired by her example, grateful for her credibility and moved by her and her mother's passion to make a difference and help others. I feel blessed that I have had the opportunity to work with her over the years as we crossed paths in access to justice work, but most importantly it's an honor to call her a friend.

In 2020, following George Floyd's murder, we collaborated weekly on a social justice event for almost a year with the goal to build the largest social justice organization on the planet. This mission excited me because I've faced injustice. I've personally been subjected to poverty, homelessness, abuse, and discrimination. I've been paralyzed twice and told I would never walk again, lived on my own at 14 years old, dealt with my mom dying two months after I graduated high school, dealt with the medical system throughout her cancer, and with raising my siblings. I faced the challenges of being a single mother in a wheelchair for 11 years, being homeless, and assaulted. Through all this, my thinking, choices, and mindset made all the difference in the world. It contributed to me walking again, becoming Ms. Black California 2003, Ms. America 2011, owning my businesses, raising two wonderful boys, and all of the other accomplishments I'm so dearly proud of. When there is more social justice, there can be more access to opportunity.

I don't know if it's because of all the challenges I've been subjected to and overcame, but I've always been inspired to help others and empower them. From speaking with the National Black College Alumni (NBCA) Hall of Fame to being featured on Historically Black Colleges and Universities (HBCUs) College tours to Andrew Young's Emerging Leaders initiative, and Call to Woman Hood I have been committed to amplifying social justice. From panels with C.T. Vivian and other civil rights activists and community leaders to helping my church and community with projects, I feel it is a responsibility to open the doors of access and opportunity for everyone, particularly those in the greatest need. Serving on boards that focus on helping women and children, like Phenomenal Women Inc., supporting organizations like Habitat for Humanity, Boys and Girls Clubs, NAACP, Southern Poverty Law Center, American Civil Liberties Union, and ADA, I long for solidarity among all who love justice and equality. I believe to do this, we all need to get *Legally Savvy*. Our communities need this and it is one step in the process that we can **all** do!

We've all been subjected to things in our surroundings that can make us feel like victims. Life is full of ups and downs, happy and sad moments, stressors, and life events. Bad things do happen to good people.

Sometimes we bear the brunt of things that we have no control over such as race, the color of our skin, poverty, our religion, family situation, our zip code or an accident. It would be very easy to become a victim of our circumstances and continue feeling sad, scared, angry, frustrated, or lost. But, instead we could choose to deal with injustice differently by being legally savvy. Taking more control of our lives and our choices allows us to live more freely, make better educated decisions, be empowered, worry less, live more, level the playing field and give life to the words on the Supreme Court, "Equal Justice under the Law."

I feel this book is so important because it provides insight into how we've been priced out and uneducated on the systems in place to empower and protect us. If you don't know your rights, you don't have any. Furthermore, if you know them but don't have access to them, what good are they? *Legally Savvy* helps people start to think differently about these issues and unlocks some of the power of the legal system and the law. This is so important because law isn't logical, it's legal, so we need to think differently. The concepts in this book can be applied to all areas of your life.

Even better, it's an easy read. I love the stories, entanglement of history, social justice, and thought-provoking ideas. Despite the title *Legally Savvy*, this book is less about "legal" and more about life. It's amazing how many profound and systemic inequities we deal with and how being legally savvy changes your mindset to improve your entire life. It helps you face the plethora of challenges that are just a part of everyday life and brings awareness to issues that we all will face. This book is a game changer!

"Don't get ready...stay ready."

Zarinah leads and lives by example. The world is a better place with her in it. She has sacrificed so much for her cause, and I love her passion to help people. The *Legally Savvy* Movement is here. Zarinah and I share a goal to see that no community is taken advantage of simply because they lack the resources the super wealthy have!

Zarinah, thank you for being vulnerable and selfless in pursuit of your purpose and illuminating these principles to change people's lives!

Please continue to make a difference. I'm looking forward to this book having a global positive impact and your second book!

—Tracy Broughton
Ms. America 2011
Social Justice Advocate, Entrepreneur, & Mother

Introduction

The law impacts everything from the relationships we have to the art we produce. The super wealthy already know this. The rest of us have to catch up!

That is what this book will do for you. It is for those of us who did not grow up with the wealth and resources to regularly connect to attorneys and receive legal advice and support. It is for those who want to get the target off their back and off the back of their communities. As an attorney, I have had the opportunity to get specialized knowledge on how the system works. In my role as a community builder and activist, I began sharing this information with small groups and then at seminars around the country.

And then I was encouraged to write this book. So, I am finally putting down my lawyerly wisdom on how to be legally savvy. This is the advice that my closest relatives, friends and colleagues have been privy to, and my clients and attendees at my seminars have heard over the years. They have told me that it has made a difference in their lives, making them more confident. It has helped them dodge some bullets in love, business, and with their finances. They have better discernment as they navigate life. Further, it has helped them confidently and proactively use attorneys to their benefit.

There are two main objectives for this book:

- to help you live a more vibrant life by increasing your legal savviness like the super wealthy; and
- to help you make the boss moves, incorporating regular access to attorneys in your life.

Refer to this book often and definitely prior to any major decision you plan to embark upon such as starting a new business, buying a home, or beginning a marriage. You will find these principles are timeless and useful in every sphere of life.

If you properly apply them, they will change your life. You will save time, money, and your sanity as you navigate the American legal system. This book is not a history book or a book of laws. It is not filled with fancy legalese so it takes a law degree to understand. This book will not make you a lawyer, but you will know you are getting legally savvier by the more insightful questions you are able to ask your friends and family at the next holiday barbeque and in how you understand and think about how to approach your life.

So, that is what this book is for. It is a new approach to speaking about our legal system in a way that all of us can digest. This is a book about principles - guiding principles that the wealthy have been acculturated to and about which the rest of us have been kept in the dark. This book will unlock these secrets. These are winning life hacks that when adopted and practiced can help you more astutely navigate life, love, business, and everything in between. Further, these are fresh tips to help you upgrade your mindset to be the boss in your life, protect yourself, practice self-care, avoid costly mistakes, and live a freer and more fulfilling life.

If you reside in a country outside of the United States, gracias, shukran, dankeschön, asante, and thank you for joining us in the *Legally Savvy* movement! It is a global movement where we support more access to information democratically shared with the people. Keep in mind the particularities of any laws here may or may not apply to you. But you can still apply the lessons to your region or country. The principles shared here are universal hacks to help you live a more empowered and vibrant life.

I believe that the more the entire community grows in knowledge the higher we all can go. No longer should access to this knowledge be kept in ivory towers under lock and key for the super wealthy.

I look forward to connecting with you and hearing your aha! Moments. Let us keep in touch.

"The Constitution doesn't belong
to a bunch of judges and lawyers.
It belongs to you."

— Anthony Kennedy,
Supreme Court Justice

CHAPTER 1

Becoming Legally Savvy

Let me upgrade you.

— Beyoncé

I love being an attorney! I am one of those people who went to law school to help people. But I am fed up with the agony many people in our community have to endure because they do not know their rights or have access to attorneys to protect themselves.

Those who grew up with great wealth, we are talking the Rockefeller types, had the privilege of having lawyers accessible to them to get the guidance to make wise decisions and avoid costly mistakes. The benefits of those decisions trickled up to them, their children, their family, and their communities."

But what about the rest of us — those of us who were not raised with unfettered access to attorneys? We wing it the best we can and suffer the consequences. These consequences trickle down to us, our children, our families, and communities. Some results turn out in our favor while others leave us battered and bruised, in some cases, permanently.

Playing by the Rulebook

In any society, there are a set of rules. Some are folkways, unwritten yet understood customs dictated by a community or society. They may raise an eyebrow if bucked or contravened. They may not land you in jail. But they may carry consequences in the spiritual realm or affect how you will be treated at the next family dinner.

There are also the rules in society that carry civil or criminal consequences. These are called laws and the consequences of breaching them can impact you in both tangible and intangible ways.

We often learn the folkways at the dinner table or when interacting with our familial and community elders at the religious center or during holidays. Many of us can relate to this because when someone does not seem to behave with an acceptable level of decorum, we often say that they lacked home training.

Well, if we agree that we learn about the societal rules or folkways at home, when and how do we learn about the rest of the laws that have a profound impact on us as well?

For most of us, we learn it the hard way. We learn it after life has smacked us in the face. We learn after:

- Purchasing a car from an auction that was fraudulently advertised as having 50,000 miles on it but it actually had 200,000 miles on it.
- Being served with cease-and-desist orders from our previous employer for starting our own nursing consulting business in our city, unknowingly violating the non-compete clause we mechanically signed upon acceptance of that job.
- Being arrested at a routine traffic stop where we carelessly consented to a search of our car and the police officer seized a bag of meth paraphernalia our last rideshare passenger left behind.
- A close relative passes away without a will and leaves us to untangle the clutter and chaos that was left behind.

- Coming up with thousands of dollars to hire an attorney to get the charges dropped from our daughter's record because she and her college roommate were roped into a dicey situation.
- Being served an eviction notice for failure to pay rent when we were just rationalizing that we could withhold rent from our landlord until he fixed the plumbing in the bathroom.
- Divorcing a narcissistic manipulative spouse who left us holding the bag for the debt she sneakily accrued behind our back.
- Marrying and sponsoring a convincingly kind, romantic, humble guy from a fascinating country that we are on their financial hook for the next ten years despite finding out he defrauded his way into our good graces for citizenship in America.

Instead of getting guidance ahead of time to avoid the headache, heartache, and the financial whooping that can come from life *getting legal*, we wind up learning our lessons the hard way - after the fact. And, unfortunately, that may be too late.

These are hard lessons. It can feel discouraging, dispiriting, and even hopeless. But this book is designed as a life hack or a manual with the principles that will help you feel empowered, informed, and primed to take on the world.

The thing is, no single person goes into a marriage imagining it will have a messy ending. No teenager starts a new school expecting to be bullied. No new graduate starts their first job expecting to face discrimination. But, life happens.

There are legal ramifications to almost everything we experience - when a baby is born, buying a house, raising teenagers, driving, starting a business, working a job, putting out artistic content, signing a deal, aging, or dying. The philosopher Jim Rohn said, "the same wind blows on us all." However, the legally savvy approach life differently. They are hopeful, but they plan for the inevitable curveballs that the winds may throw at them.

In my legal practice, I noticed a disturbing trend. I realized there were so many people coming to me way too late or not coming at all because they did not understand how an attorney could help them. They came after they had botched an attempt to handle a matter on their own or after they had realized their *hope and see* strategy had proven unsuccessful.

Another fundamental reason people were coming to me way too late is that they were checking their wallets before they were checking their rights. So many in our communities have been price locked out of access for so long that we automatically figure we just cannot afford relief. That is no way to live! So, I think we are due for an upgrade!

Traditionally, we do not get the same access as the super wealthy. We have seen it time and time again in a variety of situations. The coronavirus pandemic further exposed these disparities. We know what happens when people have access, for example, to medical knowledge and healthcare and what happens when they do not. Those who have it fare better.

Essentially, we are all probably one or two degrees of separation away from someone who suffers from a medical condition or even died because they could not afford the best medical treatment. That person was not able to get to the doctor early enough or visit with the specialist they had read about who is in another country simply because they did not have the funds.

Plain and simple, those without access are more susceptible to having minor conditions unnecessarily escalate. For example, the wealthy can treat their family member's abnormal cough better than an uninsured family and they can catch it before it turns into full blown pneumonia. On the flip side, and with all the best intentions, when the rest of us get that cough, without access, we wind up bringing Tussin to a pneumonia fight!

Healthcare literacy and access to the healthcare system are tools of prevention, empowerment, and peace of mind. It is the same with legal issues! Many of them are preventable. So, if you could catch more legal issues at the "cough" stage rather than waiting for them to become legal "pneumonia," wouldn't that be nice? You would have more peace of mind and confidence as you make business, career, financial, and relationship choices.

In this era, many of us are already looking for the hacks to make life easier — the upgrades. The pursuit of life, liberty, and happiness has been a preoccupation of ours in America for centuries. Living life fully, having genuine liberty, and being happier are our favorite categories of New Year's resolutions. This shows up in our downloads of the newest mobile apps on meditation, the latest diet or the hottest workout, sites that promise the fastest route to finding love, or that offer tips to getting richer.

With all the talk of leveling up our lives, there is one area that, if leveled up, would significantly upgrade our quality of life. But we rarely think about what that is. So, here it is. As you improve your physical health, mental health, finances, and relationships, you also want to make it a priority to upgrade your legal savviness. It is like having the street smarts the super wealthy have.

Like the rest of us, the super wealthy have family members who get sick, pass away, and have business problems. But, what they have that the rest of us do not have is legal savviness and access to attorneys that affords them a heightened degree of peace of mind as they experience life's challenges. Those who have not grown up with exorbitant wealth or are the first generation to acquire wealth, have suffered the consequences and reduced opportunities of not having the chance to be legally savvy. It saddens me because it shows the stark divide in mindset and access between the haves and the have nots.

It might even be hard to believe how some Hollywood stars who have the money to get good advice face some of the same problems as those of us who do not have their robust bank accounts, like passing away without a will. But, I'm not surprised. Just because someone has money today, if you were not raised with it, you likely did not have the advantage of developing a legally savvy mindset. So, there are more than we think in the same boat.

I am writing this book because I see the hurt and pain that kind men and women have endured who come to me after living through such suffering. As an attorney and active member of the community, I have been blessed to be someone that people come to for assistance and guidance. What saddens me most is that by the time people have come to me, it is often after a transaction gone bad. In some cases, it is a business transaction gone wrong. In many cases it is a matter of love that has rammed a knife in their heart. In those instances, it is not just the heartache and distress that one is dealing with, it is also the legal quagmire from which they now must become untangled. Sadly, it is usually not pretty. Sadly, it is usually not a simple fix. Sadly, they are often unaware of how to navigate the legalities of what will follow.

Seeing good people in a crisis fires me up because, often, there were ways that some of the distress could have been avoided if they were privy to the right information. You see, every game is played with a set of rules. While life is not a game, there are certainly rules and learning them is the first step to understanding how to master it. What if you could master those rules? What if you could live more confidently? Be more self-assured? What if you could feel prepared and not scared? That is what reading this book will help you do.

What Legally Savvy Is

Being legally savvy means having two things:

- One, an informed awareness of the underlying legalities that are linked to our daily lives, and
- Two, knowing how and when to utilize one of the most powerful tools in our society, attorneys.

What Legally Savvy Is Not

In this increasing era of incivility, I do not preach empowering people with this information so that they can behave as entitled obstinate agitators. We do not want to be obnoxious pompous punks.

Being legally savvy is not a license to be:

- immoral,
- unethical, or
- a jerk.

In fact, it is about understanding our responsibilities just as much as understanding our rights.

The truly legally savvy are not boastful, they are self-assured and some of the best people you would want to deal with. They have empathy, but they are not available to be someone's punching bag. They have compassion but are comfortable at setting boundaries. Being legally savvy is about engaging in self-care, being sincere, empowered, and proactive.

> *Nobody wants to be a sucker, but most of us don't want to be tyrants. We actually do want to get along, but we do not want to be played.*
>
> *-Dr. Ramani, Psychologist*

My goal has always been not just to learn for me and my family but to see our communities become systemically improved. This book will help us get there.

There is a degree of legal savviness that is required to live a better, more enriched life. But becoming legally savvy is not a given, it is a choice. Perhaps at one time you chose to learn karate or how to use a weapon. Well, learning how to navigate the legal aspects of life is another self-defense skill we need to cultivate. If you were not raised to be legally savvy you have to decide to acquire those skills - to learn, to exercise this "muscle" and to know how and when to flex it.

I argue that the more legally savvy we all become, and when we understand how to get regular access to attorneys, the better our society will be. It will help to keep in check those in our institutions and social settings who are predisposed to overreaching and help those who are predisposed to being silent to know when to lean in.

In the final chapter, I will also share with you some tools on how you can have access to top notch attorneys that will not break your bank.

This guide will teach you the hacks and principles to develop and empower yourself with a legally savvy mindset to navigate life, love, and everything in between. The higher your legal savviness quotient is the better you prosper.

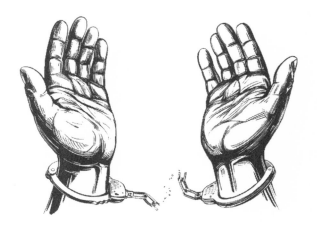

Now is the best time to launch into your legal savviness upgrade! This will positively impact the rest of your life and be a game changer for you, your legacy, your family, and generations to come.

Legally Savvy Hacks

The Legally Savvy know…

✓   Having access is a key tool of prevention, empowerment, and peace of mind.

✓   Many legal issues are preventable.

✓   To catch issues at the legal cough stage rather than waiting for legal pneumonia.

✓   The higher your legal savviness quotient is the better you prosper.

✓   That there are underlying legalities linked to daily life.

✓   When and how to use attorneys.

✓   It is not about being a jerk but about self-care and setting healthy boundaries.

When you know better you do
better.

— Maya Angelou

CHAPTER 2

Destigmatizing Access to the Legal System

Knowledge is power. Information is liberating.
Education is the premise of progress, in every society, in every family.

— Kofi Annan

I f you are like me, for a variety of reasons you may never have spoken to or consulted an attorney until you were an adult. Perhaps you:

- Were not raised that way.
- Presume your situation is not serious enough to get an attorney involved.
- Are a nice person and see no need to rock the boat.

Or, perhaps, by this stage in life, you may have had a scrape or two with the law that was so bad that you felt forced to get help from an attorney. But you saw it as your last resort. If this sounds familiar, welcome to the family!

> *Does using the assistance of an attorney feel:*
>
> - *uncomfortable,*
> - *intimidating,*
> - *embarrassing,*
> - *mystifying,*
> - *weird, or*
> - *just plain aggressive?*

I understand. But it is time to flip the script on this type of thinking! It has not served us, but rather it has harmed us or someone we care about. When a way of thinking has harmed us, even though we held it out as a universal truth, it is wise and prudent to upgrade it with better information. That is what this book will help you do.

Being legally savvy should be a fundamental skill we all get to acquire in the same way that we learn to read, write, and do math. Understanding the intersections between daily life and the legal system, what attorneys do, why you need them, and when you should call one should not just be an exclusive privilege of the super wealthy. That has generated too much imbalance in society. It is almost as if being legally savvy and using attorneys has been conveniently stigmatized for the rest of us. This trick has left us vulnerable and at a serious disadvantage where we are 'hiking the same mountain' as the super wealthy, but someone has 'hidden our hiking gear!'

> *The history as to when using attorneys became an exclusive privilege of the elite is reserved for another book and another day. The past is what it is, but as we stand here today, enough is enough!*

We have to deal with the reality that we have been generationally conditioned to not embrace understanding the legal system. We have shied away from understanding it, to the point that we are intimidated by it and as such, are not protecting ourselves or getting out of life all that we can.

I get it! Talking about the law can be oh so boring! Statutes, rule books, and old white men are not most people's taste du jour. If we wanted to discuss judges, we would much prefer it be the ones on *American Idol* or *the Voice* instead of the Supreme Court of the United States.

One of the main explanations people offered to me as the reason they crossed law school off their list of career paths was "you have to read a lot there, don't you?" It was often accompanied by a facial expression that looked as if they were chewing on some bitter fruit. In case you were wondering, yes, there was a lot of reading. And, yes, lots of it was boring. But not all of it. The law is vast, and it continues to grow.

I have heard it all before, from men and women over my years as an attorney:

- "I don't need to call an attorney because I am a good person," or
- "I'll wait and call the attorney. I don't want to start a fight," or
- "Ewww, why is she speaking to an attorney?! What did she do wrong?!"

I know what they mean. I have said those things before because I did not grow up with attorneys all around me either. These are comments the rest of us have become accustomed to saying. But I have news for you. The super wealthy would not utter such words! They operate from a completely different paradigm when it comes to life, its intersection with the legal system, and use of attorneys. That paradigm has helped them stay wealthy and enjoy other benefits of life.

It is important to remember that according to the Legal Needs of American Families Study, "Americans forgo or avoid legal help because of cost, access, and trust issues" and "93% of respondents believe lawyers charge too much for their services." The traditional model to access the legal system is complicated and cost prohibitive for so many of us to use attorneys the way they are really meant to be used.

According to the 2019 World Justice Project, "People face a variety of obstacles to meeting their justice needs, beginning with their ability to recognize their problems as having a legal remedy. Indeed, fewer than 1 in 3 people (29%) understood their problem to be legal in nature as opposed to "bad luck" or a "community matter." That is why we must work on increasing our legal savviness. We need to be able to recognize more quickly when an issue may have a legal component.

I went to law school to help remove barriers. But pragmatically, I knew that to run a business money had to flow. And so, with the very people I went to law school to help, my fees became a barrier to them accessing justice.

During my traditional solo-law firm practice I had a case that I will never forget. A woman came to my office to get help on a much needed domestic relations issue and I quoted her the retainer needed to get started on her issue. Of course, that figure had a comma in it. She looked down at an ornate ring on her finger which could have been a family heirloom and told me she would take it to the pawn shop and return with my money. I felt so grimy, like a heartless mob boss.

Busting Limiting Legal Beliefs

1. *Only failures need lawyers.*
2. *Lawyers are more interested in winning than in justice.*
3. *If you hire or consult with a lawyer, you will end up in court.*
4. *Lawyers are more interested in money than in serving or listening to their clients.*

> 5. *Lawyers are not active members of the communities that they represent and so cannot understand the context of members' lives.*
> 6. *The legal system is deliberately complicated and stacked against the average Jane/Joe. It only represents those with money and power.*

Do not let the story end here for you. These are thoughts that have stifled the rest of us from getting the help we deserve.

Retaining A Lawyer Does Not Mean Automatic or Costly Litigation

Consulting with an attorney does not mean filing a lawsuit. Attorneys are also known as counselors. The attorney can advise you on how best to handle the situation. They will tell you what options you have and help you weigh the pros and cons of each. Taking this route and having this knowledge will help you avoid making a wrong move that may cause you some legal backlash or just plain embarrassment. I have been in that spot and I am an attorney. I was happy I got consultation to avoid looking ridiculous.

This point is powerfully illustrated in a situation that faced Tracy Broughton, Ms. America 2011. Tracy was recovering from a car accident that left her paralyzed. She was building a custom home and needed her doorways widened so they would be wheelchair accessible. As a leader in disability rights advocacy, Ms. Broughton knew a lot more about the Americans with Disabilities Act (ADA) requirements than most of us. From her studies she figured that the builders had to enlarge her doorways. But before she spoke to the contractor, she astutely contacted her attorney. Her attorney advised her that the ADA regulations she was thinking about did not apply to residential property. As an alternative, the attorney suggested she could just ask nicely, which she did. The builders agreed to widen the doors and, fortunately, Tracy was able to save face and still get what she wanted. That is the power of good advice!

Where It Began for Me

From the time I was young and raised by woke parents who grew up in the 1970s in New York to working in community development in Arizona and nationwide since I was a pre-teen, I have seen the ramifications multiple communities suffer because of inequities. There were and are issues of racism, white supremacy, social and economic justice, gender discrimination, religious xenophobia, and remnants of colonialism.

I was nearing the end of my undergraduate studies. I marched. I convened and participated in diversity dialogues. I knew societal change was necessary and I wanted to do my part. I was majoring in Spanish and unofficially minoring in Arabic and sign language with thoughts of becoming a professor or a United Nations diplomat. But it was not until one haunting day that my path would change as I understood that legal access was an inextricable piece of the puzzle. It is a piece without which the entire puzzle falls apart.

My senior year of undergraduate college coincided with the terrorist attacks on September 11, 2001 that included two planes intentionally flown into the World Trade Center in New York. Tuesday, September 11th was a tragedy for all Americans and for other nations who lost citizens in the attacks across the country. However, the measures taken both immediately and in the longer term directly targeted and impacted some communities in America disproportionately. The aftermath for Muslim Americans was on a whole other level. Akin to the treatment the Japanese-American community faced after the bombing of Pearl Harbor, our community was targeted. Many members were investigated and pressured by the FBI as well as harassed and attacked as scapegoats by violent Americans.

At that time, I was the newly elected Vice President of one of the most active student-led organizations on one of the largest university campuses in the country. I was also a co-leader of an organization instilling leadership capacity in dynamic young women. Being in a leadership position from a young age and being in that campus role, I was thrust into the media and was privy to conversations where I received startling stories from lay members of our community as well as activists that members of our community were being arrested and detained by the FBI.

It echoed scenes from the 1960s when African American leaders such as the Reverend Dr. Martin Luther King, Jr., Malcolm X, Fred Hampton, and other community members were being surveilled and attacked by the FBI.

This is a powerful law enforcement agency in the United States and so it is important for any member of the community to interact with these agents only with the benefit of an attorney to ensure that their rights, including due process are not violated and to ensure that those without power are not entangled or entrapped by the state with its access to unlimited resources.

But, many community members were not aware of that. There were decent members of our community facing serious legal consequences for making seemingly inconsequential missteps when interacting with the FBI. Some thought, because they sincerely had nothing to hide, that it was no big deal to invite the FBI agents in for tea when those agents knocked on the door without warrants or subpoenas.

Some were asked about people who may have attended their mosque and mistakenly mentioned they did not know that person rather than stating more precisely, that they did not recollect that person, or better yet, decline to answer those kinds of questions at all without more information about why the FBI agents were asking. These types of understandable errors in judgment ensnared community members into lengthy legal trouble.

I saw that those members of my community and even I needed to up our awareness about the law. We needed to become more legally savvy! Many community members did not have experience utilizing attorneys so that they would be skilled at facing the oppression heaped on them from society. Members of the community did not have ready access to justice. Their mindset was inexperienced with the law.

I thought back on our march chants of "no justice, no peace" and it became clearer how these two concepts are linked. A non-lawyer activist can only go so far. But, when that activist needs help, they need a lawyer. I was being called onto a new path to help bring about true justice so our communities could experience true peace. And so, I made the decision that the next language I needed to learn was the language of the law. This would enable me to intercede for my community.

Later, I would learn that in courts, lawyers are, in fact, the **only** ones who are permitted to enter the chambers of a courtroom to represent another. But at this stage, I had enough to know that understanding and navigating the law was an essential tool in this country. So, like many attorneys, I went to law school to address the civil rights injustices and oppression that so many of the rest of us face out in society.

But there were other earlier influences that also shaped my legal life. My mother, a skilled social worker and dynamic university professor, started Black History Month in my elementary school. She had opened my eyes at a young age to issues of social justice, and to the oppression people, often women and children, face at home. As Dr. King, Jr. said, "Injustice anywhere is a threat to justice everywhere." And so, in my legal studies and practice I focused on those laws that impacted relationships and families.

I realized that oppression can occur even in our regular, everyday lives, such as when dating, getting married, or having children. I saw that these seemingly simple, common, life stages can trigger changes under laws and regulations that can wonderfully protect you or horribly wound you. I learned it was important for us to be legally savvy to navigate love and life.

Fortunately, as my experience practicing law went on, I never lost my passion for teaching and for seeing systemic change. It only deepened.

In practice I saw two glaring truths. Firstly, I saw that clients who came to me or were sent to me (either by referral on from my work as a government attorney) came as a last resort. Secondly, I noticed that people would come to me way too late. I was presented with numerous scenarios.

> I would see the single father who attempted to modify his child custody arrangements with the court on his own. However, he filed it incorrectly. The court still cashed the check for the filing fees, and he had to do it all over again.
>
> But by this point he had missed a critical window to make his objections known and was no longer able to file his objections.

The saying, it is never too late, unfortunately is not always true. Especially when we are discussing legal matters, it can definitely be too late. There are rules in the law called statutes of limitations or SOLs. These are the timeframes within which your grievances can still be brought to a court for relief. Ronald Jones, a partner at one of the top law firms in the country, while helping a group of entrepreneurs retain this essential fact, left the crowd with the unforgettable zinger: "There are SOLs so if you ignore them you can be SOL." He had me rolling! But it is so true. Delaying addressing legal issues can leave you in distress and with fewer options on how to address them than if you had handled it earlier. Your options are dramatically diminished, kind of like how stale bread can really only be used as breadcrumbs. You also may be left with only a very costly solution.

This really disheartened me, and I went on a quest to figure out how to help more people have the knowledge and legal access that they deserve. I regularly found myself in a position to help decode and make sense out of the legal process that a girlfriend, family member, or community member was going through. So, just like my love for Spanish and other languages, I became the Legal Translator.

Then, I knew this needed to be scalable. I knew that people without a lawyer in the family or an accessible close friend in their network were at a disadvantage. Additionally, I knew that times have changed and lots of people have legal matters that can be more complex spanning multiple areas of law and even across multiple states. The rest of us deserved to have on-call ready access to attorneys to truly have the assistance that is needed to live better.

I love for people to not just go along but to understand the bigger picture. There are some things that are out of our control. But there are some things we can do to make life easier. I love to see people elevated to live an extraordinary life and to break free from the shackles of a life of ignorance. Sadly, there are those who know how to work with the system and then others who get worked over by it.

I decided to liberate myself from the traditional practice of law to reveal secrets most lawyers cannot tell you or will not tell you. Unfortunately, most attorneys' livelihoods are predicated on untangling you from your messes. Having a certain awareness about the law and knowing how and when to incorporate legal consultation into your life can reduce your need for costly legal assistance further down the road. This is key. It is like getting an insider tip.

If you have questioned why others have fared better than you, often it comes down to a knowledge issue and knowledge comes down to an access issue. Simply put, they often fare better than you because they have better intel than you. Better intel is what wins wars. And, while I am reluctant to call this a war, if you have been on the back end of a legal issue you have felt the battle. Legally Savvy is about arming you with the tools and armor to face the day, to deal with the matters of life and matters of the heart that can slip into the realm of having legal implications.

The Legal Needs Study shows "that legal problems know no economic boundaries. All income levels experience legal issues or events at about the same rate - 66%." But the legally savvy can address them better.

Understanding the legal implications of life is like a muscle that needs to be exercised. Just like working out helps us to keep our bodies sharp and agile, learning these tips here will help keep your brain sharp and agile. Also, it is no fun being played. It can happen at any age and any stage of life. It does get worse as we get older because many never have learned this skill in our younger days. And when we get older we often get cozy in our private world, delay leaving our comfort zone and can be easy marks for con artists, scammers, and just plain old meanies. But as long as you are still breathing it is never too late to learn to be more legally savvy. Though it is certainly better to do it sooner rather than later.

Take the *How Legally Savvy Are You Quiz* on the next page.

Legally SAVVY QUIZ

How Legally Savvy Are You?

Answer "Yes" or "No"

Did you have an attorney review the last contract you signed, including online terms and conditions?

Do you have a signed and notarized will and powers of attorney (POA)?

If yes, have you updated your will and POAs in the last 5 years?

Do you know if you live in a community property or common law state?

If the police stopped you for a traffic ticket and asked you to pop your trunk so they can take a peek, can you refuse their request?

If you are starting a business you consult with an attorney before you get the LLC?

If you get married you talk to an attorney before adding your new spouse to your previous home deed?

Do you have a law firm that you regularly consult with prior to making life decisions?

If you are arrested and want to remain silent do you know the magic words to use?

Having your apartment lease reviewed before you sign it is ideal?

Now, tally your results!

If you have:

8-10 Yes's: Congratulations you are legally savvy!

5-7 Yes's: Good job. You are moderately legally savvy but can get more out of life.

1-4 Yes's: Ouch, you're getting duped! But fret not, there is hope!

Knowledge is not power, it is only potential. Applyingthatknowledge is power. Understanding why and when to apply that knowledge is wisdom!

-Takeda Shingen

CHAPTER 3

Lawyers Aren't Just for Bad Things

"We have a complex system of government.
You have to teach it to every generation."

— Sandra Day O'Connor,
Supreme Court Justice

I recognize that you may have to read this section a few times because it is advice that flies in the face of good old solid lore. But here goes, lawyers are not just for bad things. In fact, lawyers are equally, if not more, for positive aspects of life. This is principle numero uno.

If you are coming to an attorney when something bad has happened, you are probably too late. There are probably several steps that have been missed that could have prevented the issue from getting so bad. Unlike JLo, Mario Lopez, and fine leather, legal issues do not get better with time. "You have come to me too soon," said no lawyer ever! Most of us attorneys wish we could have helped you much earlier on.

Understanding this alone will save you time, heartache, and money. It is one hack that will help you conquer the proverbial half of the battle and may be the single most significant differentiator between the super wealthy and the rest of us. This principle is simple yet profound. It is the golden rule. It is the bedrock, the foundation, the quintessence of becoming legally savvy.

I know that hearing this may be jarring and causing you some cognitive dissonance. I know that the narrative in most of our communities is quite antithetical to this because I grew up in those communities as well. We have been raised to think the exact opposite - to believe that lawyers are just for bad things. Unfortunately, this trope plays out often in our media and we have come to believe it as much as we unfairly believe all women love pink or all men love blue. In our minds, we were taught to believe that the only time you need an attorney is in catastrophic situations that we should just try to be good and avoid.

This is a common misconception around the less wealthy and those who have not been raised with wealth, that you only use attorneys when someone is being arrested or being sued. Situations like:

- Uncle June Bug is going to jail, or
- Some megalomaniac tries to sue you in some wayward business dealing, or
- You are going through a nasty divorce.

Here is the cold honest truth, whether you are good or bad there are laws that are impacting you. Many of the laws are in place to protect you. If you are reading this book, you are likely one of the good ones. Bad things happen to good people. And a lot of good happens to good people. Simply put, the earlier you are aware that the law is all around you and how to handle the law, the better you will fair, the more vibrant life you will live.

The challenge is that the rest of us have little to no experience adequately handling legal matters, so we are not skilled in recognizing the subtle stages a situation takes from good, to mildly irritating, to downright horrible.

Why You Really Need a Lawyer

Attorneys are required to undergo regulated education, examination, background checking, and licensing requirements that must be renewed annually. We can refer to an attorney as a lawyer, esquire, or in Europe as a solicitor or barrister. But, as we discussed earlier, one of my favorite names for an attorney is counselor at law. They listen to you and are obligated to counsel you as to what is in your best interest.

Attorneys are like the best friend you could ever have. Attorneys are licensed professionals and are certainly held to upholding the state law, the U.S. Constitution, and the ethical requirements of their governing bodies. So, within those walls, they are to guide you as to what is best for you. This is why you may see a scenario where two spouses may each have their own separate attorney. The advice as to what is in one's best interest may not be the same for the other.

Attorneys are the best at keeping your secrets too because of a universal ethics code called attorney-client privilege. There are specific ways to trigger this privilege. You cannot just start venting on a crowded train about your life, find out an attorney is in the seat next to you and think you have invoked an attorney-client relationship carrying that privilege of confidentiality. You should not just send an email with details about your issue to an attorney. No! It is best to reach out to an attorney privately and request a professional consultation with him or her. In most cases, when approaching it like that, the fact that you even placed that call to the attorney is confidential even if it turns out you do not end up getting that consultation.

When we understand that attorneys are not just for bad things, we can begin to really live a more vibrant life. For example:

- Have you ever wondered if you could turn your large social media following into deals with major brands? Discuss it with your Entertainment attorney.

- Maybe your friends have loved the specialized cakes you have made for the last bridal showers in your crew, and you wonder if you can make it a viable part-time gig. Discuss it with your business attorney.

- Or, you have been working on an original screenplay and you want to know how to protect it before you shop it around to producers? Discuss it with your intellectual property attorney.

These are delightful occasions where your creativity has been sparked. We want to keep the positive light shining on you. Consult with an attorney at the idea phase. Get counsel on some of the pitfalls to avoid early on and the suggestions for how to make it successful if you decide to follow through.

The other advantage of consulting with an attorney is that special attorney-client confidentiality we discussed earlier. You do not have to fret that after sharing your idea with your lawyer, you will see the exact same project implemented and designed up the street because your lawyer told someone about the idea.

Friends with Benefits

Going into business with a friend or family member can also be loads of fun and rewarding. Having a family business is a dream for many. Even going into business with your three best friends could be a childhood dream come true. Just imagine, if you are going to make it big, how cool it would be to get to walk the beaches of the world with your friends. Hey, it worked out great for Mark Zuckerberg and his college friends, right? So, this is a fun time, but also one of the best times to consult with an attorney. Get advice on how to make sure the friendship survives the business.

Consider the situation of two upwardly mobile friends:

Sasha and Emma were getting ready to launch a side business together. It was to be a partnership between the two of them investing equally and sharing the profits equally.

Emma, because her family was well to do, had her attorney draw up the contract for them to sign. She gave it to Sasha to sign. Sasha was the first generation in her family to acquire wealth as she had been a successful dentist for about five years.

Sasha and Emma got along great. She was pumped about the prospect of starting this business with her talented friend. But Sasha thought she should have an attorney look over the contract just to be responsible and to ensure she understood all of the key terms.

Interestingly, as the attorney reviewed the contract, he conferred with Sasha to confirm this was supposed to be a partnership. Sasha affirmed that it is a partnership agreement. Then to Sasha's surprise, her attorney told her he was glad that she had this contract reviewed before she signed it. As it turned out, it was not codifying a partnership agreement but rather establishing a sole proprietorship in Emma's sole interest!

Needless to say, Sasha ditched the agreement and as you can imagine promptly ditched the friendship as well.

Prior to this contract review, this sensational business idea was moving along smoothly. The two friends were getting along so well and were days away from putting their respective financial shares into the pot for their business. Things were going "*good.*" Fortunately, Sasha did not wait until after she signed the contract and put her money on the line for the business to consult with an attorney. Had she done so, she would have likely had a difficult time combating the validity of their contract brandishing her own notarized signature. This signature, bearing witness against her and locking her into lining her friend's pockets, would be hard to overcome. And let us even give Emma the benefit of the doubt. Let us assume that, by some fluke, Emma unwittingly handed Sasha a contract for a sole-proprietorship. Even if it was an honest error, to revise the documents once signed and the business has already started rolling, would be a mighty task, and an expensive one too.

These are business activities. But, what about the happy occasions in our personal lives? We will discuss more broadly the various legalities you have to know about our love lives. This book includes an entire chapter just on the romantic relationship because it is one of the most common and troubled areas that I see people encounter. So, let us take getting married for a quick example. This is one of the happiest times in a person's life. For a girl, she is finally able to have a day all about her, shop for her dream dress, rally her best friends to be her bridesmaids, and to have the chance to have multiple pre-wedding parties in her honor. The last thing she wants to think about is boring old law.

> *There was a young woman, Rene, who figured before she went too far she should place a few calls to an attorney because her fiancé, Harris, was previously married and now divorced. The thing was that Rene's fiancé was not married civilly, he was only married according to his religion in North Carolina.*
>
> *But here's the rub. The couple moved to Texas to live. In that jurisdiction there is a variation of common law marriage still in effect. Over simplified, common law means that despite not having a marriage license from your state court, if you live as a married couple for a certain period of time and hold yourself out to the public as a married couple then you are recognized as married.*

> *Harris said that he and his previous wife got divorced religiously. But he did wonder if he had met the threshold of being legally married in Texas and as such had to effectuate a divorce in Texas courts. Rene made some phone calls and spoke with a family law attorney in North Carolina and a separate family law attorney in Texas to track down the answer. It is a good thing she did because if her fiancé had still been legally married her marriage would have been invalid and he would have been a bigamist.*

Other Positive Scenarios That Could Require an Attorney

There are loads of good things that you may have the fortune of going through such as adopting a child, expanding your business with employees, signing to play college or professional sports, being invited to showcase your art at a studio, inventing an app, starting a humanitarian project, starting a new job, retiring from a job, or even volunteering to take the neighborhood youth group kids to a swim party.

> *In 2013, Idris was retiring from his job at one of the biggest banks in the country. The bank was downsizing during the prolonged aftermath of the 2008 recession. Idris was offered a severance package and given several days to look it over. It was standard practice for his HR department to suggest that the employee have an attorney review these documents before signing.*
>
> *Idris took them up on their suggestion to have the materials reviewed by an attorney before he signed them. It was a good thing too because the package was a set of documents that when signed opened doors to certain compensation and closed doors to others.*

> *Idris was able to have an attorney looking out for his best interest so when he signed the package, he knew exactly what to expect for his retirement and how much his wife would be entitled to so they could manage their next chapter peacefully.*

Humanitarian work is some of the most rewarding work in which one can engage. I am a proponent for community service on various levels be it local, interstate, or international. Serving on the board of your house of worship, starting a STEM youth camp, building a women's shelter for domestic violence survivors, volunteering your medical skills to the free clinic, or even starting an animal rescue for stray puppies are laudable. And I imagine, if you are reading this book you have popped into some community service organization. But unfortunately, I have seen too many times when altruism popped a person right back in the face.

> *Aniyah was volunteering with a community-based youth group when she was a new college graduate. It was summertime and one of the volunteers had a great idea to take the children on a field trip to go swimming at a community member's house. They had a sparkling blue pool equipped with a slide and jacuzzi. This was a brilliant idea because the summer was exceptionally hot and most of the children in the group did not have ready access to pools.*
>
> *Fortunately, Aniyah, while she liked the idea, figured she would call an attorney to see if there were any liabilities she should keep in mind if they decide to take the children to the pool. The attorney was happy she called because she advised Aniyah that absent some kind of a waiver, she could be opening herself up to some major liability if something, God forbid, went awry that was completely out of her control.*

That is why being legally savvy about community service is a smart thing to do as well. Again, it is not about being scared, it is just about being prepared.

Even buying a house or buying a car are prime reasons to consult with an attorney. When you are making boss moves like these you definitely want an attorney having your back. Firstly, these are some of the largest purchases you will ever make in your life. So, the stakes are high. You are putting a lot of money in or you are on the hook for a major time and financial commitment. Even if you are renting or leasing, have those contracts reviewed. These are some of the best times of your life. Know what you are agreeing to so that it does not become a nightmare. Know what you are responsible for and do not sign anything you do not know how to get out of. This includes marriage contracts! We will discuss this further in a later chapter.

Remember, lawyers are not just for bad things but can assist you in avoiding bad things. So remove from your vocabulary, 'I hope I never need an attorney' and replace it with 'I wonder what an attorney would say?' Join the ranks of the super wealthy who know that legal situations can be just as good as they are bad and get the guidance to make the best decisions.

Remember, attorneys are counselors and have expertise in different areas. Just like doctors have specialties, lawyers also have areas of expertise and specializations. Resources will be shared in the last chapter on how to find the right lawyer to match the situation. So, just as you would not have a podiatrist check your heart, you do not want a tax attorney handling your copyright. You want to consult with the best attorney in the area you are seeking help for. Utilize them to help keep happy times happy.

Legally Savvy Hacks

The Legally Savvy know…

- ✓ Lawyers are not just for bad things.
- ✓ Unlike JLo, Mario Lopez, and fine leather, legal issues do NOT get better with time.
- ✓ Being legally savvy in life, love, business and community service is just a smart thing to do.
- ✓ To have contracts and agreements reviewed before signing them so they know what they are agreeing to and what they are responsible for.
- ✓ Not to sign a contract they do not know how to cancel or exit from.
- ✓ That instead of saying 'I hope I never need a lawyer' they say 'I wonder what a lawyer would say about…'
- ✓ That attorneys have specializations and to use the right attorney for any given situation.

If one really wishes to know how justice is administered in a country, one does not question the policemen, the lawyers, the judges, or the protected members of the middle class. One goes to the unprotected--those, precisely, who need the law's protection most!-- and listen to their testimony.

-James Baldwin

CHAPTER 4

The Deck is Stacked Against You

Truth never damages a cause that is just.

— Mahatma Gandhi

When we look at the numbers, there is no wonder why the rest of us have not been experienced at the legal system or normalized to use attorneys. Most of us do not know lawyers. In my 2003 entering law school class, we were only five African Americans students, four accomplished ladies and one gifted brother.

According to a 2015 Washington Post editorial, law was the least diverse profession in America. Not much has changed since then. According to the American Bar Association Journal, in 2019 there were approximately 1.33 million active lawyers in the United States. That means that about .4% of the United States population are actively engaged in the practice of law.

- "Eighty-five percent of active attorneys are white,
- Only thirty-six percent of attorneys are women,
- Just five percent are African American or Black,
- Just five percent of them are Latino,
- Only, two percent identified as Asian,

- Two percent identified as multiracial, and
- Just one percent as Native American."

That means that the vast majority of attorneys are, surprise, surprise, white men! So, the likelihood of even having ready access to attorneys in our networks or communities can be slim. Then when we consider comfort levels with professionals in terms of whether or not they understand our experiences and perspectives, we can start seeing the layers of barriers.

Diversity of the bench has long been an issue as well. Judges are attorneys and if the attorney population is not representative, the judges are not either. Most judges do not reflect the entire population. What that means is coming before a judge who has shared our life experiences is slim. While they rule based on the law, much of what a judge can do is discretionary, and they bring to the table their bias from their life experiences. Many judges do not have experience with non-majority family structures, religious practices, mental health sciences, or diverse cultures. So, you will see that some judges are known for alternative forms of sentencing, like community service and others are not. For example, I know of a judge who wisely ordered community service with a Muslim relief organization for the woman who vandalized a mosque in her area while other judges habitually heavily criminalize episodes that occurred while a military veteran was having a PTSD mental health crisis. Again, we can see how the deck is stacked against us. If the judges do not know us or interact with us, their gaps in experience impact our judicial outcomes.

'Alleged' Equal Justice Under the Law

Race

Racial disparities exist at virtually every point of the criminal justice process. We need only watch the evening news to see the contrasts in how the justice system impacts white people versus African American, Indigenous, Latinx, and other people of color.

As I write these pages, a few short days ago, on January 6, 2021, the United States Capitol was stormed by a group of radical white insurrectionists. They were there contesting President Joe Biden's election victory which made Donald Trump one of the few one-term Presidents in the history of the United States. This was the worst siege on the Capitol since 1812. Many of these people were armed and extremely dangerous. They boldly pushed back barricades disobeying direct commands to cease and even assaulted police officers. In fact, one officer died as a result of the mob violence. They steamrolled their way in desecrating the senate floor, one of the major arteries of the United States government. One shirtless thug, donning a furry hat with horns plopped himself on the very chair the Vice President of the United States just sat moments before presiding over the certification of electoral college votes for the next president. It was entitlement run amuck and quite frankly highly disturbing. Several of the news outlets showed one of the white male insurrectionists beating a police officer with a big American flag pole.

Large portions of the mostly white mob chased the police officers down and pushed them out of the way. Very few arrests were made that day. They were literally attacking the police and were not even shot with the exception of one woman, who was shot as she, along with the mob, were attempting to breach a different entrance to the capitol. It did not take people of color one second to recognize that African

Americans have been shot dead for much less. African Americans have stood unarmed on a street corner and have been murdered by the police. And, if this mob had more melanin in its complexion, the restraint exhibited by the law enforcement would have been a far cry from what this white mob received.

Like many firsts this year, this was one of the first times in my lifetime when I heard so many white people publicly acknowledging the disparity in treatment between them and people of color. They did not need to have a commission convened to study the abhorrent inequality. No statistics were needed, although there are plenty, to show the disparate treatment people of color receive from law enforcement and the court system. This time, it was plain as day.

They did not have to conjure up a hypothetical example to contrast with because only a few short months earlier, in June 2020, a large Black Lives Matter protest against racial injustice in the wake of the brutal murders of George Floyd in Minnesota and Breonna Taylor in Louisville, Kentucky was met with severe force by the police. That protest was not even close to pushing back barricades or entering the Capitol. However, they were treated like they were a mob seeking to overthrow the government! As time passes, we are seeing arrests made from the January 6th insurrection. It is reported that family members and friends are providing tips to assist the FBI in locating those participants. Ladies are even employing popular dating apps to catch some of the guys who are bragging with photos of themselves at the Capitol. But, time will tell if the overwhelmingly white insurrectionists will face justice. The woman who was caught on national news absconding with Speaker of the House Nancy Pelosi's laptop is home on house arrest. People of color have been assessed high bonds virtually rendering them bondless for much less and stay locked in jail awaiting their day in court.

The United States is experiencing a racial reckoning that has spilled over into racial reckonings around the globe, including London. I hope real change will come of it.

Gender

Due to the sexism in the country, women are compensated at 70 cents on the dollar for a man. African American women and other women of color typically earn even less than that (around 63 cents). That means that being able to access justice is a further long shot. This is just math. Men are more likely to be able to afford attorneys than women. And, white men, as a whole, have it best.

The *Me Too* movement that went viral in 2017 brought necessary attention primarily to the sexual harassment women have faced at work. But, conversations opened about all spheres of life. I wish I could tell you that today is the day our country acknowledges the pervasive white supremacy and systemic racism and puts an end to it. I wish I could say toxic masculinity was extinguished. But, sadly there is still a color of justice in the country, and it leans toward white. Men still dominate the legal profession as attorneys, judges, and law enforcement. And, it will take a long time and a lot of work to acknowledge, apologize, heal, reconcile and reform the layers of institutions that operate with underlying inequities.

Take for example, Tamar.

Tamar just knew she had a case for obtaining sole custody of her children. She had a great job. She lived in an intergenerational household with her parents and siblings. The living arrangements meant she had emotional support and physical support to help watch the children. It was the perfect scenario and the children loved being in a full house with so many people to play with.

> *The judge disagreed.*
>
> *When she went to court she was shocked that her ex-husband Kurt was awarded primary custody. The judge decided that Tamar's intergenerational living with her parents and siblings meant she could not manage her children on her own.*

It is outrageous, but these things happen all of the time. Consider the case of Laila.

> *She called the police because she was experiencing domestic violence from her partner. It was not the first incident, and the abuse had consistently escalated. She managed to get to the phone and call 911.*
>
> *The police came and arrested her and her husband.*

So, this hack is a critical one though I wish it were not true, but, here goes: Be aware that the deck is stacked against you. The race card, gender card, and wealth card are regularly played in this system. I hope this hack will eventually need to be phased out. But, given how deeply entrenched, and systemic the biases are, I expect otherwise.

If you fail to understand this and unrealistically manage your expectations around this, you are sunk. I would be leaving a piece of your armor unsecured if I did not add this to the list. As it stands, the playing field is not level. It is uneven and it is not fair.

There are well-intentioned, honorable, and conscientious members of law enforcement and the judiciary. I am honored to have several of those individuals as personal friends and colleagues. Many of them would agree it is still an uphill battle we face to bring true the promise of "equal justice under the law" etched into the Supreme Court building into everyday reality. That is why the best course of action is to learn to be a legally savvy gatekeeper. Learn how to prevent interactions with the court systems as much as possible. The court system is a slice of the entire legal pie. It is wiser to use the other safeguards and tools the legal system affords you, such as those discussed in this book, to avoid the court systems. An ounce of prevention is worth a pound of cure. The best defense is a good offense. Do your best to insulate yourself from confronting these institutions and then manage your expectations if you wind up forced to deal with it.

Additionally, work on a different, broader term of winning because fair will likely not be on the table. For example, you may take comfort in the fact that your case went swiftly, or that it is finalized and you do not have to see your opponent daily. Try to find a silver lining so you can have peace and move forward.

If you are still angry, that is understandable. Consider seeking a woke counselor you can vent with, get validation from and tips to thrive through it. Additionally, if you are willing to get socially or politically active, you can channel that anger constructively to lobby the legislature to pass better laws that reflect a deeper understanding of diverse communities and what women and minorities go through.

For example, over the years, the laws around domestic violence have been broadened. But it is still not enough. In addition to the emotional duress that accompanies these relationships, when someone can finally muster up enough strength to leave these relationships the system can be a cold lonely mountain to climb. Today, at least there is a concept of marital rape, however in the not too distant past there was not before. Wives were expected to never turn down sex from their partner. Their spouse was entitled to sex from their spouse whenever they wanted it and they were justified in taking it. Fortunately, today, there are legal protections and no means no whether you are married or not. So, lobbying can work.

Consider joining a community action network or starting your own to bring purpose and direction to your pain. Finding a purpose could even be a personal win going back to school, attacking your bucket list, or even radical self-acceptance to affirm you are more than enough. If you have an experience where you found purpose out of your pain, I would love to hear about it and perhaps share it with the *Legally Savvy* community.

De Facto Segregation

The reality is, America is still highly segregated. Despite the laws that desegregated our society in the 1960s, our society is still de facto segregated. Communities live in their little enclaves. It has been said that Sunday is the most segregated day in America where people go to their monochromatic church congregations. Mosques in America are ethnically more mixed, but as this community grows, the separation by ethnicity or language can also be starkly observed. The more distant we are from one another, the more disdain can develop between groups. Conversely, the more proximity we share with one another the more compassion we can foster. We do not know each other, and the polarization has only deepened in the last few years.

A Pew study showed that, people were more likely to marry across ethnicities before they would marry across political party lines. The legal system is a product of its society. It reflects its values and priorities like a mirror. Our society has yet to address head on the inequality and as such layers of challenges, like discrimination, still occur.

Raise the Bar

What about just having more members from our community go to law school and become attorneys to bring this information to us and represent us. That's easy, right! Well, let's look at the numbers.

According to the US News and World report, the average cost of law school currently is $40, 244 for full-time residential students, compared with $46,161 for those out-of-state per year. Law school is a 3-year degree program following a bachelor's degree. So, not including the costs of obtaining a bachelor's degree, one would have to figure approximately $120,732 or more to go to law school in your own state.

Law school is competitive, especially to get into a ranked law school. So, it is usually advisable to apply to multiple schools to increase your likelihood of being accepted in that year you are applying and each of those applications come with an application fee. You want to figure in the costs for taking the Law School Admissions Test also known as the LSAT, a preparation course to prepare for the exam or materials to study on your own. If you do get accepted to a school that is out of state, tuition costs increase as well as your living expenses because you may need to rent an apartment, have a car with which to commute, or Uber expenses to add to the budget.

Just imagine what you could get for $120,000 – an Aston Martin, the Roots to play at your birthday party, or rent a private jet three times! And, a quick search on zillow.com could find you a condo or a modest town home for sale in Winston-Salem, North Carolina or Rochester, New York that you could flip to a rental property. So, we are talking about a sizable investment.

Then, upon completion of law school you will have to figure in the costs of taking the bar exam to actually become a licensed attorney. Without passing the bar exam you are a person who graduated law school, but not a lawyer. In some states you may not even write your degree, Juris Doctor (JD) after your name without being licensed.

So, to give yourself the best shot at passing the bar exam you will be wise to pay for a bar preparation assisted study program, which is about $2,000 according to BarBri, one of the leading bar review programs. Then to sit for the Bar exam in, say my home state of Arizona is another $1,040. In Florida, it ranges between $600 and $3,000 depending on whether you applied as a law student or a more seasoned attorney. If you want to practice outside of your home state you may have another Bar exam to take and prepare to cover the costs of being waived into a state with reciprocity.

Well after that, you will figure annual fees and continuing Legal Education courses required to keep your license active. So going to law school and pursuing the route of an attorney is no walk in the park.

At orientation as a 1L, my law school dean said, "Not every smart person needs to become a lawyer." I agree! I believe we need diverse, conscientious talent in all spheres of life from medicine, to social services, education, home making, politics, Wall Street, and Hollywood. Far be it from me to tell someone to pursue a path about which they are not passionate. I would much rather see someone pursue their passion and kill it! But I am also a huge proponent of more community members entering the law. We need more diverse members of our community as attorneys and in other spheres of law enforcement. When a lot more of us enter this field, we can shift the status quo and make accessibility more of a reality. More networks would have someone in their family who can shed light on these very important issues.

But let's be real, when we have our community members graduate from law school, the community starts to look for "homie hook ups" and free legal help. Well, as you can see, that brand new lawyer has a six-figure nut to crack to get above water again. So, we are going to have to respect our community members who do pursue this career. There is only so much pro bono they can do before they need pro bono! And just like you expect to be paid for your training and for doing your job, attorneys deserve the same right. See, I have never been a proponent for lawyers being free. If law school were free, then we could discuss attorneys being free. I do not foresee that happening any time soon.

Part of these expenses associated with just the law school aspect accounts for the $300 to $400 an hour fees attorneys charge. The fact that attorneys charge these rates is not the issue, I believe. The profession is expensive, and the work is hard. For a lawyer to guide someone through the legalities of their current life often takes research, regular meetings with the client, conferring with other attorneys, and putting their license on the line to advise the client.

However, it is important to remind ourselves that this is not a reason to just go it alone and dispense with attorneys. At the bottom of every self-help form it says to consult an attorney for legal advice. The reason for this advice on the forms is that there is no one-size fits all in legal matters. While we may have some similarities, we have enough uniqueness which has to be factored in. So, even if your friend checked a particular box on the same form you need to fill out, whether you should do the same for your circumstance is a question for a lawyer.

The main issue is that the majority of the rest of us do not make anywhere near $300 to $400 an hour. I share resources in the final chapter of this book with alternatives. But, for the most part, individuals are responsible for raising their own legal fees. Government attorneys, also known as public defenders, are only assigned if you are facing loss of your physical freedom such as jail time or facing the loss of your children if the Department of Child Safety attempts to remove them from your home. Other than that, you do not get an attorney appointed for you and paid for by the Government.

This means that you do not get an attorney assigned for you if you are facing an eviction, domestic violence, a child custody matter, handling a business dispute, or even a speeding ticket. I say all of this as a reminder that legal access is an issue.

These are some of the reasons why I encourage you to become legally savvy. Learning how to proactively consult with attorneys while a matter is still good and positive will hopefully prevent you from being on the receiving end of one of those costly situations gone bust. Except for rare circumstances, you would rather not have to resolve an issue in court. Most attorneys will tell you, going to court should not be seen as the first resort. It is the last resort. That is because there are too many variables that occur when facing a trial such as:

- Who is the judge and is she woke? Hint: She likely is not.
- Who will be the members of the jury and are they woke? Who knows!

Going to court is just too much of a crapshoot, and I do not advise gambling with your life. Add on top of all of this the systemic racism and sexism that is woven into the fabric of the court system. Court can be like a box of chocolates; you never know what you are going to get. So, the least amount of time you must use the court system to get matters resolved, the better. This also improves the chances of you living a more peaceful life. That is what I wish for you. Not to cower down and be some person's or even society's scapegoat. But, rather to have the tools to protect yourself early on, to learn how to be a gatekeeper deflecting drama from creeping up into your life. It is so much better to keep drama out rather than trying to excise it out.

If you do have a situation where you do have to engage the court system or law enforcement, get proper legal assistance as early as possible and then hold your head up high. Keep the faith, be as prepared as you can, and go for it. Perhaps the fact that you simply stood up will begin to make that ripple effect to make things better. Maybe the next person after you will have a better outcome because you showed up first and helped to open a judge's eyes.

Perhaps nothing like that will happen. This is the real world where there are not always tidy happy endings. But, you can take pride in the fact that you stood by your principles, suited up, and handled the issue with grace. At the end of the day, justice will be served one way or the other. God don't like ugly.

Focus on controlling what you can control and lean into your spirituality, supportive family, and supportive friends. Someone who got away with taking advantage of you will have their day of reckoning. Forgive yourself, go easy on yourself. Speak the kindest to yourself and refuse to let anyone steal your soul.

Legally Savvy Hacks

The Legally Savvy know…

- ✓ The deck is stacked against you.
- ✓ There are layers of institutions that operate with underlying inequities.
- ✓ Not to gamble with their life but to be a proactive legally savvy gatekeeper.
- ✓ Use attorneys sooner rather than later to avoid court.
- ✓ The court system is a slice of the entire legal pie. It is wiser to use other safeguards and tools the legal system affords you to avoid the court system.
- ✓ This is the real world. Manage expectations accordingly.
- ✓ To work towards social change and/or find a personal purpose.

Education is the passport to the future, for tomorrow belongs to those who prepare for it today.

- Malcolm X

CHAPTER 5

Magic Words

Real magic is not about gaining power over others:
It is about gaining power over yourself.

— Rosemary Guiley

Just like the tales we heard when we were children about the magic words that once spoken, opened an otherwise locked door to a buried treasure, this can also work in real life. The magic words are not "abracadabra" or "open sesame" which works great in fairy tales. But, in real life, there are words that, once committed to memory, will seem like magic because of their effects. These words open doors where only a brick wall or stone appeared before.

The effects appear to be magical to the rest of us, but not to the super wealthy. To the super wealthy who have been lawyered up for generations, these words are just a part of everyday vocabulary. The rest of us have been in the dark about this information for so long that it seems as mystical as one-eyed Willy's treasure laden pirate ship or Indiana Jones's treasure map.

In real life, when we talk about the doors the magic words open, we are literally talking about opening up opportunities to raise our families in peace, opportunities to be the boss of our lives, receiving necessary relief to a problem we may be facing, or de-escalating a situation with child protective services or the police. These magic words may also save your life.

Have you ever been in a situation where you thought you were handling it but you didn't get your desired outcome? You are very certain you were speaking very clearly and passionately, but the person on the other end was not giving you what you needed. There may have been much time wasted and blood pressure elevated as a result. I have seen emotions range from irritation to desperation. You can encounter this in a variety of scenarios.

- For example, my friend used to work for a major bank and he would tell me stories of customers who would call in to the bank to complain about an overdraft fee that was assessed to their account. The bank customer would complain about it and ask my friend why it ended up on their account. The conversation would go back and forth, often ending with the customer hanging up frustrated and the overdraft fee still intact.

  My friend told me that person probably wanted the overdraft fee waived. However, since the customer did not specifically *request a waiver for the overdraft fee*, my friend was trained to not extend it as an option.

- Another friend who worked in customer service for an insurance company during the coronavirus pandemic said something similar. She revealed that if a customer called for help making their payments but did not specifically say they were requesting a *hold on their payments due to economic struggles caused by the Coronavirus pandemic*, then customer service could not offer that as an option.

Understand that articulate speech will not get you anywhere. Save your breath and your time. So, here is the hack:

- Know that there are magic words.
- Learn them.
- Use them.

Knowing this will help you to be more legally savvy, encouraged, and less depleted.

History of Law Enforcement

The history of law enforcement in the U.S. is complex. At the time our Constitution was written and set the foundation for the new government, slavery and the disenfranchisement of women were practices protected by law. Amendments including the 14th, the equal protection clause and 19th, extending voting privileges to women, were passed about 100 years later.

The U.S. legal system is complex, multi-faceted, and multi-jurisdictional. It has many crevices and crannies that continue to perpetuate systemic racism and inequalities. While some laws can seem to change overnight, beliefs may lag, especially when you are talking about centuries of acculturation. Further, the roots of policing, in the U.S. evolved from individuals who were enforcing the abhorrent practice of slavery. They were given broad authority to ensure African American people, who were viciously enslaved against their will, were kept under those repugnant conditions. Law enforcement was also misused to perpetuate genocide and displace Native Americans. Over time, the laws around racism and the police force evolved. But, sadly, some people have not. Enough have wanted to keep things like they were in the "good ole days" and some continue to misuse the powers of this institution to carry out their personal racist, sexist, power and control agendas. Sadly, this can be observed in all institutions of the U.S. because those institutions were founded upon inequality. Black people and people of color do not only get snuffed out on the streets by police. They also get snuffed out in the boardrooms and ivory towers as there are enough people still in charge there, as well, that are acculturated with racist, sexist, and power and control agendas. It is just as suffocating, but the difference is that it is bloodier when the police are involved.

The fact that the United States tops the chart for having the most incarcerated people in the entire world says something. The fact that African Americans make up such a small percentage of people in America yet comprise one of the largest groups incarcerated says something. More effort needs to be made to bring about our more perfect union.

Law Enforcement Training

Most men and women who join the police force are there to do their job like the rest of us. However, since many of us have infrequent interactions with police and because of the horror stories we have seen, we do not really have a good idea of what legitimate policing looks like. So, let me debunk some myths about the police.

Not every police department is created equal. There are about 18,000 different police departments in the U.S. and there is no universal training in which every department must participate. Each department is subject to different laws, codes, and as such, different standards. Therefore, police training varies.

There are some countries, like Finland and Norway who require their new police cadets to attend their country's three-year police university and graduate with a degree equivalent to a bachelor's degree. The education and skills acquired is similar to the academic rigor someone going into nursing or education would be expected to undertake.

In the United States, not so much. For example, the U.S. Minneapolis police department, the one who employed now convicted murderer Derek Chauvin, has a 16 week training for rookie cops before they are armed and sent on the streets with a mentor for 6 months.

Police training in the U.S. ranges from 10 weeks to 36 weeks. Some departments get quality diversity training and some do not. Some departments receive regular training on mental health issues and some do not. Some departments have community advisory boards made up of leaders and active community members to prevent and address community challenges, some do not. (See below for further discussion of community boards).

Generally, the training and education in law given to police officers is limited. The laws which they enforce are complex but the areas of law in which they train are finite. Some departments do a thorough job of teaching about the constitutional roles of the police and rights of individuals, others do not.

Law enforcement officers are trained on how to gather information and investigate. They listen, observe, ask questions, and are trained to use a variety of other tactics to solve crimes. While using physical torture in interviews and interrogations have been banned in the U.S. for years, psychological tactics are still used.

Dealing with Law Enforcement

Knowing the magic words to say in all areas of our lives is important. This includes situations when dealing with law enforcement. Knowing when to be silent is important. The phrase "your words can and will be used against you" are not merely a catchy introduction recited during the beginning of a Law & Order episode. They possess meaning and consequences empowered by the Supreme Court of the United States.

I cannot tell you how many times I have come across a case where my client's statements came back to bite them. I know they were thinking they had nothing to hide, they were good people, or they were just trying to be helpful. This could all be true. But these clients were still missing some fundamental information the rest of us also usually fail to realize.

It is important to know that you may not be aware of everything that is going on around you and your statements may not be contextualized the way you intended. You need to understand that your statements can and will be used against you. When we are dealing with law enforcement, a good rule of thumb is to never talk to them without your attorney present. Your attorney is experienced enough to know why the questions are being asked, if you should answer them, and how it may affect you later. There are too many blind spots, for the average person, when dealing with law enforcement. You want an attorney to help navigate you through that maze.

Remember that being legally savvy with law enforcement comes down to understanding more broadly what the role of police is and is not, the magic words to which they are legally bound to and trained to respond, and letting go of unrealistic expectations.

It is understandable why we are baffled in this area. With law enforcement, whether it is the local city police, the sheriff's department, county public safety officers, the Federal Bureau of Investigation (FBI), or Immigration Customs Enforcement (ICE), our culture has a complicated relationship. On the one hand, we love our shows and movies featuring our favorite cop squads. I will admit Captain Olivia Benson and her SVU Law and Order crew, the Bad Boys for life, Will Smith and Martin Lawrence, and the international super cop duo Chris Tucker and Jackie Chan hilariously portrayed in Rush Hour are my favorites. You may have yours. In Hollywood and in real life, we love to see good cops bringing down the bad guys and justice being served. What we do not like to see is bad cops getting the good guys and an injustice occurring. We become angry and disillusioned when we see instances of law enforcement misusing their badges with no care or accountability.

Many of the barriers and disparities that block the path toward better policing can be traced to a history of discriminatory and racist policies, the impacts of which continue to be felt today. Institutional defects in the construction of police and society overall created and continue to cause problems. In the U.S. we tend to over criminalize activities and underfund known crime prevention measures such as education, and mental health and substance abuse treatment. The relationship between police and society is strained.

Enforcement and Community Mental Health

The role of the police has evolved from strict enforcement into doing multiple jobs they are not trained for and that are more aptly suited for trained social workers or other mental health professionals. The only resource for assistance that many of us know is 911. The result is we call in the folks with guns for help with a depressed family member rather than a counselor who can recognize and deescalate a mental health episode.

Community Awareness

Our citizens are not informed about their rights and responsibilities. Because of the lack of education and information, we do not really understand the scope of police work and what they can or cannot do. Very few of us have attended a police academy or participated in a drive along with our local police department. In the wake of popular legal dramas such as Law & Order and CSI, people have a skewed dramatized view of how the system should work. All of this is a messy convergence that is undermining the integrity of our justice system.

Policing and Community Boards

As mentioned above, some departments have community advisory boards made up of leaders and active community members to prevent and address community challenges. For example, in Arizona, there are a variety of community advisory boards. One such board, on which I serve, the Arizona Muslim Police Advisory Board was formed in 2001. I know of times when we have worked with the Phoenix Police Department, the Chandler Police Department, the Maricopa Police Department, and the Peoria Police Department to clear up cases where a Muslim community member may have been involved.

> *A few years back, there was an incident of a man claiming to be Muslim who attempted to storm a highly secured facility. When he was apprehended by police, the man began ranting about his religious beliefs that drove him to do that act.*
>
> *As a result of the relationship that had been built between the arresting police department and the Muslim Advisory Board the issue was handled appropriately. The police did not blow the incident out of proportion in terms of suggesting it was a terrorist threat, but rather dealt with it appropriately as a sick man needing help.*

The relationship between the police and the community also helped to mobilize preventative safety measures following the aftermath of the mass shooting massacre in the Christchurch Mosque in New Zealand when our local Muslim communities in the U.S. were under high alert.

There are some departments with leaders doing it right. They are focusing on community engagement and attention to the law. Nevertheless, in my opinion, now is a prime time for all police departments, like any major institution, to rigorously re-examine their policies and procedures and reform where necessary. Such reform is essential to eradicate any legacy of discriminatory practices that can adversely impact the community they serve and the fellow colleagues they serve beside. If you can attend a community board in your area, get involved. Take advantage of those opportunities to learn and share your perspective on what makes a safe society.

Roles and Responsibilities of Law Enforcement

So, let's talk about what you can do – that includes understanding who the police are, what they can do, and what your rights are.

I know that there is disparate treatment that we should not have to deal with. But the reality is we live in a society still stratified by race, gender, and wealth, among other things, and it can be dangerous.

To be legally savvy is to know this and prepare for it. In addition to access to attorneys, we and our families need to know and understand our rights, and what law enforcement can and cannot do.

Law enforcement officers do not make law. With some discretion, they enforce the laws made by their local councils, and state or federal government, including interpretation by judges of those laws in case law. The areas of law pertaining to carrying out policing duties include maintaining peace in the public, investigating crimes, making arrests, and enforcing laws.

Unlike attorneys, police are not trained to give personal counsel on how those laws can work in your best favor or not. Nor when they give advice is it protected or privileged confidential communications between you and them. Their roles are totally different. Their job is public safety and enforcement of laws. This is a critically important distinction to understand. Failure to understand this has often caused people to stumble hard.

After you become more legally savvy you will begin to cringe when you see movies or hear of people asking the police for personal advice. "Should I talk to you, Mr. Policeman?" The police are going to say yes, of course! That helps them in their investigation. But that is a question for your attorney, not the police investigating a possible crime!

There was a young man who received a business card for a police detective at his door telling him to call the police.

When he called, he asked if he should bring his parents with him to the station. The officer said no. So the young man went down to the police station alone and figured he could just clear up the situation by talking it out.

The questioning intensified and the next thing the young man knew was that he was getting arrested. He ended up being imprisoned for 10 years.

While you are obligated to tell the truth, law enforcement officers may legally lie to you to induce you to divulge information. Although, there are some movements around the country to put a halt to this sly practice, particularly when investigating juveniles because it has led to false confessions, it is a common, effective, and legal police tactic.

For example, say you are being interviewed by police about a recent burglary in the neighborhood and the interviewing officer tells you that your roommate had already pointed the finger at you as the one who broke into the house. But the police may not have even met your roommate yet or your roommate may have said nothing of the kind. The psychology behind this deceit is that if you did break into that house your conscience will weigh on you to come clean and blurt out a confession. At a minimum, what may start happening is that you begin talking in an attempt to defend yourself or explain "your side" of the story. Either way, you start sharing details that the police think may be pertinent to solving the case.

I certainly advocate a peaceful and safe society where true threats are investigated and apprehended. However, when you aid in an investigation you do not want to be naïve about the role of the police.

Our roles and responsibilities are like a three-legged stool – we have a responsibility, the police have a responsibility, and society has a responsibility to see that justice is carried out. Being legally savvy means you can separate fact from hyperbole. It means you can distinguish solid policing from overreaching. And it means you can do your part to avoid the kinds of rookie mistakes some of us make that often end up in avoidable muddy puddles the super wealthy and legally savvy avoid.

Our Role

In a nutshell, and I recognize this might sound crass, to be legally savvy, avoid opening your mouth and telling your business to law enforcement without attorney guidance. I understand how difficult it may be to follow this advice because of our history. We have been taught that asserting our rights is rude. I have especially heard this from people who are more recent immigrants to the United States. Their parents may have come from countries where police corruption is the norm and are in the United States to live the *American Dream* of economic prosperity. They have taught their children to keep their heads down, to work hard, and to be cooperative and compliant. So, if they interact with police, they often talk way too much.

Take the story of Imran.

> *After the September 11th attack, the FBI contacted many members from the Muslim community in America for interviews. In some cases, the FBI called and invited the individual to their office. In other cases, the FBI just stopped by their home unannounced.*
>
> *In Imran's case, a couple of agents just stopped by his home. The agents identified themselves as FBI agents and asked to come in for a quick chat. Having nothing to hide and not wanting to look guilty, Imran welcomed them in and offered them tea.*

> *At first Imran was happy to help and the agents seemed quite friendly asking him about the origin of ethnic artwork he had decorating his living room. But he noticed the questioning started to feel more like an interrogation and he could not get the agents to leave.*
>
> *The agents stayed for four hours questioning him about the people he knew, who he had seen at the mosque, where he had been and with whom he had traveled.*
>
> *The agents mentioned his immigration status and the fact that they knew he was up for his citizenship status. This had Imran worried and intimidated that if he did not help, he might not get his citizenship approved.*
>
> *From time to time the FBI agents continued to arrive again and ask Imran more questions. After going through a few rounds of that Imran finally reached out to a lawyer.*

But, even for those who have long historical roots in this country, when we see a badge and a uniform, we get antsy. We have seen enough examples of police brutality in cases where it seemed like someone was doing everything right and still got killed. Remember, Philando Castile? He was fatally shot by officer Jeronimo Yanez in 2016 during a traffic stop. He was required to let the officer know he was armed and licensed to carry. As he was doing that, the officer fired seven shots close range and killed him.

There is a real toxic history between some communities and law enforcement. The result of it has left even the strongest person with major anxiety when they see police coming toward them.

I have heard a highly successful, well dressed young African American man living in the suburbs with a master's degree and an upper-level white collar job say he almost spilled hot coffee on himself one day when he thought the police were following him.

Regina King, one of the most famous black actresses and directors in Hollywood, remarked at the 93rd Oscars awards in April 2021 that despite her wealth and fame, she too fears for her black son when he leaves the house.

Sunny Hostin, an attorney, former prosecutor, and co-host on the popular day time show, *The View*, recently said that she felt at times more comfortable with her black son being in South Africa on his mission trip than in his native United States of America. Wealth and education are not bulletproof shields if a cop is bent on abusing his power.

One world famous comic joked that he too had concerns as he was only "up close famous" implying that he would also be antsy of police.

It seems like there is nothing we can do to prevent being mistreated by a rogue cop. Sadly, that is probably true. Do your best to create a record that you did not provoke them, say a prayer, and have faith someone caught the transgression on video.

We all hope and pray we are never subjected to a brutal use of force encounter with the police. But there are other circumstances where we can do our part to prevent getting ourselves into unnecessary sticky situations. There are still everyday things we should know and do when interacting with law enforcement and this includes using the magic words.

> *One wintery morning in a Midwest city, the local police showed up at Nina's front door. The officers said her name appeared in a police report and they had come to see if she had more information about the person they were investigating.*
>
> *Because it was cold, she invited the police officers inside and proceeded to answer all their questions. Nina was happy to help and knew that since she had not done anything wrong, there was nothing to worry about.*
>
> *After reading this section, is there anything you would have done differently?*

Let me be clear, any time you interact with law enforcement or police, be respectful and polite. It is their responsibility to de-escalate situations, but you do not want to come off defensively. Being respectful does not mean waiving all or any of your rights. You can be respectful and assertive at the same time.

If police or the FBI show up at your door, do not invite them in. You do not have to invite them in nor are you being rude if you do not. They are not there for a social visit, no matter how cordial they seem. "No chai for the FBI" is a catchy slogan the civil rights organization CAIR stamped on tea mugs for the community to remember. It is sage advice when dealing with all law enforcement entities.

Legally, law enforcement are only permitted to enter your home with a written warrant signed by a judge. If they have one, call your attorney at that moment and ask for their help to assist you in verifying the warrant and that everything in the warrant is in order. Ask the officers to slip the warrant under your door or press it to the window so you can review it. What you must understand is that when police enter your home, they are observing the entire surroundings of what is in plain view and if they have a warrant, they are authorized to search anywhere that item could presumably be hiding.

If they approach your home and do not have a warrant, you can step outside your house and close your door to speak with them.

Keep the conversation limited.

This has nothing to do with whether you have something to hide or not. You have a right to privacy and from an unlawful search.

> *Chris and his older brother James were sharing an apartment off campus. Chris was James's biggest fan. James always had the best personality and introduced Chris to some great people since they were young. College life was*

busy so Chris and James did not have much time to chat and catch up. When they would they would spit silly jokes back and forth and then they would be off again to class. One week James would return home to the apartment with some cool items and give them to Chris as a gift or say it was for the apartment. One day it was a 42 inch Smart TV for the living room. Another day it was the new Apple watch. The next time it was designer sunglasses. Chris did not think much of it even though he knew they were both on lean college student budgets. The gifts were nice and James always looked out for him since they were kids.

Well, one day, while Chris was home alone studying and James was out, two police officers stopped by the house. They asked to talk and Chris voluntarily motioned that they could come in. Once inside the apartment, the officers said they had been looking for James. Chris said he did not know where he was at the moment. But in plain view, the officers saw the Smart TV and the designer sunglasses that matched the description of items stolen from the nearby mall. They arrested Chris and as James returned home arrested him too! They were shocked!

After spending a couple of nights in jail, they were released on bail. It turned out the items James acquired were trafficked goods from the night the mall was looted! They both then were assigned Public Defenders and hoped to win their cases.

When the officers showed up to the apartment, Chris did not have anything to hide. He had been minding his business going to school and taking care of himself. But, instead of letting the officers in, the legally savvy thing he could have done was to greet them at the door, ask what they were looking for, hear they do not have a warrant and *say that he would gladly get back to them after he talks to his attorney. At that point, he could have talked to his brother and called his attorney. James could have helped him track his whereabouts and realize he obtained those expensive items at a surprisingly steep discount which could explain that they may have been stolen.*

The attorney could have helped Chris find a way to check if those items were stolen and then how to return them without incriminating themselves. Now, they both have an arrest on their records, missed school days, and burglary charges that they may have to bring up on their grad school applications and some job applications.

The impacts described in the scenario with Chris and James have collateral consequences. Retired Judge and law professorPenny Willrich teaches, "Collateral consequences most frequently affect people who have been convicted of a crime, though in some states an arrest alone—even an arrest that doesn't result in a conviction—may trigger a collateral consequence."

You want to do your best to prevent arrests. You are not expected to do everything an attorney would do, but those unsavvy moves make it harder for your defense attorney to defend you.

Being Questioned vs. Being Arrested

It is also important to understand that being questioned by the police and being arrested are two separate things. Unless and until you are read your Miranda rights you are not under arrest. But make no mistake, the statements you make prior to the Miranda rights being read can and will still be used against you.

In most jurisdictions, you must at least provide your name for identification purposes. If you are not under arrest, you are free to go and not required to answer any other questions. I will remind you to always be respectful and polite about it. Survive the stop. Be prepared, not scared. Remember the legally savvy make sure they have 24/7 access to an attorney. So, this is a good time to use the magic words, *I would like to speak with my attorney.* Once given permission to make that call, do it!

If you ever find yourself in a situation where you are being arrested by a police officer or law enforcement, you will be read your Miranda rights and just like it says you have the right to remain silent.

Invoke it!

If you choose to invoke that right, you must do more than just stay silent. You actually have to say the magic words "I am invoking my right to remain silent." Then, here is the kicker. You have to remain silent. Shut up! Silencio! Zip it!

If you continue to answer questions after having invoked your Miranda rights, you nullify that right, i.e. waived your right to remain silent.

Now would not be a good time to start yapping away in an attempt to prove your innocence. No! The legally savvy thing to do is no matter if you are innocent or not you state you invoke your right to remain silent, request your attorney, and stop talking.

Never talk without your lawyer present. I have not heard of one case where someone talked their way out of a pickle only into one.

I have heard recordings of police interviews where the police were clearly letting the person know they have the right to remain silent. The officer also asked a couple of times if they wanted to speak to a lawyer first before talking and the suspect just kept talking.

> *Ronnie was arrested for suspicion of driving under the influence. After he was read the Miranda rights, the officer asked him if he had been drinking beers. Ronnie said, nope, wine!*

These are incriminating statements that can make it difficult to give you a defense. Be mindful when giving statements to police that these can also be used in civil litigation against you.

> *Latoya was in a car accident. Kyle pulled his car in front of her. Kyle hit the brakes and Latoya smashed into Kyle's car. It had a minor dent in the bumper. Latoya jumped out of the car and started apologizing to Kyle for hitting him. Kyle was shaken up badly but he said he was fine.*
>
> *A bystander called the police and when they arrived at the scene, the police took statements from Latoya and Kyle. Latoya was sweet. She owned up to the responsibility for hitting Kyle and she got the ticket.*
>
> *A few weeks later she was served with a lawsuit for damages to replace Kyle's car and for medical expenses totaling $86,000 with a copy of Latoya's confession to the accident attached to it. Latoya hired an attorney to defend her in this lawsuit.*
>
> *Now Latoya's attorney in the civil lawsuit will have to overcome her emphatic statements of guilt in the police report.*

I am definitely an advocate for personal responsibility and generosity. But you do not want to get railroaded. Get advice on how to make amends not to be exploited. In some cases, if you are just a witness to a crime it may be prudent to also consult with an attorney prior to providing a statement to the police.

Prepare Teenage Drivers for Encounters with Law Enforcement

Along with every teenager's driver's license should be a family training about the magic words to use when encountering law enforcement. In addition to teaching children that if stopped by the police they should be respectful, keep their hands on the steering wheel at the 10 and 2 position, and survive the stop, the rest of us need to start teaching our children how to say, **'I would like to speak with my attorney.'**

They need to know it. They need to practice it and they need to have the number to an attorney who will answer at all times. Teenagers can find themselves in a situation where an officer asks to search their car or trunk. Without a warrant, the magic words are **no thank you officer, not unless my attorney advises me to do so.** <u>Not</u>, can I call my mom or dad?

Without probable cause or a warrant, police do not have the right to search your property or person. If you give them permission, then you have given them the right. **Do not give them permission.**

There were a group of friends driving home from school when their car was pulled over by a police officer. The officer was friendly. He asked to see the driver's license and registration for the driver. The driver passed along the proper information. The officer ran the information and returned to the car.

He thanked the kids and said they could be on their way but asked if they would pop the trunk for a minute. Fortunately, the teenage driver was educated by his parents and was quick to decline the request. He used the magic words, "I would like to speak to my attorney" and the officer let him call. The attorney spoke with the officer and explained she advised her clients not to submit to a warrantless search.

The officer gave the phone back and the teenagers were able to go on their way. One of the kids in the back seat was extra relieved because he had dropped a bag of marijuana on the floor, possession of which at that time would have had all of the kids arrested. The young kid driving the car was just being kind to give this other kid with the weed a ride. Wisely, he decided not to give that kid a ride again.

His parents would be so proud!

If you have children or children in your life - nieces, nephews, community little brothers and little sisters - sit them down and teach them this information. I have regular conversations with my siblings about using the magic words.

- Have any children in your life read this chapter.
- Do practice drills with them where they say it out loud so they feel prepared.

Legally savvy teens grow up to become legally savvy adults. Most importantly, they grow up.

Do You Believe in Magic?

Using the magic words, "I would like to speak with my attorney" is a game changer. These should be the first words out of your mouth. These are the words that officers are trained to respond to and **must** respect. It is enforced by the Constitution of the United States and the Supreme Court of the United States. Remember, the Miranda Rights. You have the right to an attorney.

Calling your mom, a pastor, or your friend might be of comfort, but it will not help you one bit in terms of what the police can or cannot subsequently do. So, that is not what you want to ask for first. Cut straight to the chase and use the magic words. An officer told me that whenever they hear someone has an attorney, they walk very lightly with that person and follow the rules very closely. This is what you want!

Remember that if the interaction is going beyond the question about your license and registration you need to ask to speak with your lawyer. Be respectful but say it.

It sickens me and rips my heart out when I see footage from these fatal police encounters. But, when the tape plays, I never hear the magic words being used. We do not know this critical information that the legally savvy know. And, I am not naïve. I expect not all would have been prevented, but I am convinced that if more of our community members were trained on the magic words and had a number they could reach an attorney twenty-four hours a day and seven days a week, the vast majority of the tragic stories we hear on the news and social media would not be. The violence of those encounters might have been squashed at the outset.

Calling an Attorney for non-Criminal Interactions with Enforcement

Magic words are relevant in various spheres of life. "My attorney said" are three of the most powerful magic words in the English language. Legally savvy parents, legally savvy teachers, legally savvy coaches, legally savvy athletes, legally savvy singles and so on would be wise to get proper advice and learn the terms to say.

The Legally Savvy Undocumented Mother

Alicia was a loving mom and beloved wife. She was also undocumented. For several years she and her husband David, who is a U.S. citizen, had been trying to get her status changed. It was a lengthy process so, in the meantime, they went about life.

One summer, Alicia repeatedly requested her husband David to fix the taillight on their car. She did not want to have any reason for the police to stop her. One night, while heading home late from work, the police saw the broken taillight and pulled Alicia over. Alicia's fear came true! When the police officer approached her car and asked for her license and registration, she promptly said she did not have a driver's license because she was undocumented.

She immediately asked the officer if she could call her husband. The officer said no she could not. But when she used the magic words and asked if she could call her attorney, the officer's demeanor changed. He started treating Alicia like she must have been someone important and allowed her to call her attorney.

From the side of the road, Alicia called her law firm and they immediately connected her to an expert attorney in immigration. The attorney told her she could be arrested and if so, to call back as soon as she is booked. Or, the attorney said, she could receive a ticket and if that was the case to call in the morning to strategize its defense.

Alicia got a ticket and got to go home to her children and husband that night. Although she forgot at first, she remembered in time to use the magic words and had her attorney on standby. Alicia teaches this story to others on how to be legally savvy.

The Legally Savvy Parents and the New School

There were parents who were helping their child start at a new school. The new school refused to count the honors credits from the previous school.

The student was concerned. She was a high achiever and knew that not accepting the credits meant her academic goals would be delayed. Her parents did not know if the new school was being fair or not, so they reached out to their attorney who handles education law.

> *Their attorney advised them that the new school was not following their district's policies by declining to accept the transfer credits. So, the parents were able to go back and use the magic words, "my attorney said" the credits should be approved. After that, the tone changed, and their daughter was able to start school without skipping a beat.*

The Legally Savvy Leader and the FBI

> *Jamilah was a doctor and community leader. One day while she was packing to go on an anniversary couple's retreat, she received a startling phone call from the FBI.*
>
> *The FBI asked her to come down to their local headquarters for a chat. Before accepting their "invitation" she said she was heading on a trip she could not move and would get back to them.*
>
> *In the meantime, she quickly picked up the phone and called her law firm. They connected her to the attorney versed in these matters who called her back and chatted with her. Her attorney was livid that she and her community were getting those harassing calls. But, he calmed down and told her what the FBI had the right to do and what her rights were as well. Her attorney told her that the FBI has the right to call and ask her to come down for an interview. But, she had the right to refuse. Jamilah's attorney advised her to call the FBI and use the magic words "my attorney said" I don't need to talk to you and if you want to talk to me, put it in writing.*
>
> *The FBI agent never put it in writing and probably went on to the next community member who was not legally savvy.*

The Legally Savvy Activist

José decided to join the recent march for racial equality in his city. He stayed on the sidewalk and followed the flow of the rally. But while he was out there, he got rounded up by the police and zip tied and asked to sit on the curb.

When the officer made his way back to him after putting others in zip ties, José used the magic words 'I would like to call my attorney.' The officer chuckled at first not expecting those words to come from this young student but José reiterated he had the number for his attorney. The officer let him make the call and the attorney said to put her on speaker phone.

Right there on the side of the street the attorney deescalated the situation and José was the only marcher released right there on the street.

The Legally Savvy Dad

One Friday night, at home with his wife and teenage daughter, Casey heard a knock at the door. The person identified himself as a case worker for the Department of Child Safety investigating a claim of child abuse.

A few blocks away that same night, Phil also received a knock on the door and it was a different child safety case worker also conducting an investigation. When the case worker at Casey's house asked to come in, Casey politely and confidently used the magic words asking for a few minutes to call his attorney first. The case worker agreed. Meanwhile at Phil's house, he let the caseworker in and was starting to get belligerent.

> *Neither Casey nor Phil had any idea why their home would be investigated. But Casey was able to call his law firm and speak with a juvenile law attorney right then and there. The attorney asked to speak with the case worker and found out that Casey and Phil's daughters were mad their parents would not let them go out that night and worked up a scheme to call child services on the other's parents. The case worker at Casey's said they have seen that before from disgruntled teenagers, thanked him for his patience, and left.*
>
> *But Phil did not have an attorney, was rancorous, and confused. The case worker removed his daughter from the home and gave Phil notice of a court hearing to refute his daughter's removal and his daughter spent the night in foster care.*

These kinds of cases can be sticky. It is important to investigate allegations of child abuse and neglect. I have seen horrible cases where parents abused or stood by while a partner abused their child. It is awful and those parents need to have any remaining children removed from their home and the parents need to be charged criminally.

Sadly, however, there are other cases where there is no abuse but an ex-partner weaponizes their kids against someone or tries to alienate those children from the other parent. Or there may be a vindictive and overbearing in-law who disagrees with your parenting style and makes false claims against you. I have seen children who were removed from their home on Friday nights and their parents were not able to get any answers until Monday morning. Without using the magic words and having an attorney on standby, that is the kind of limbo you can find yourself in.

Being legally savvy is a skill. Similar to any skill, to gain mastery, you must regularly practice it.

There are myriad areas of life where having the magic words are essential. The good news is, you do not have to dig out ancient ruins from the Mayans or trace your steps to the Lost City of Gold to uncover them. To learn the magic words that unlock doors in real life you just have to knock on one door – a lawyer's. There are lawyers with expertise in all areas of life. Again, sit tight for some resources in the final chapter on how the rest of us can have this kind of access.

Nobody knows when they will have an emergency, but we can all be prepared for when those emergencies arise. These tips will help you avoid catastrophes you have control over. Use this guidance to take control and be the boss in your life!

Legally Savvy Hacks

The Legally Savvy know…

- ✓ The role of the police and their responsibilities
- ✓ That being respectful does not mean waiving your rights
- ✓ That asserting your rights is not rude
- ✓ To learn the magic words and use them
- ✓ Not to invite law enforcement into your home without a warrant
- ✓ To not talk to police without an attorney
- ✓ To teach and practice the magic words "I would like to speak with my attorney" with the teenagers in your life
- ✓ That, if under arrest, you invoke your right to remain silent by using the magic words *I invoke my right to remain silent*
- ✓ To get advice and when necessary say "my attorney said"
- ✓ To have 24/7 access to attorneys for emergencies
- ✓ To remain silent without an attorney
- ✓ Zip it!

In a time of turbulence and change, it is more true than ever that knowledge is power.

— John F. Kennedy

CHAPTER 6

_____

Death by a Thousand Cuts

Details matter. It's worth waiting to get it right.

— Steve Jobs

nother issue I see as the reason we do not get the proper legal guidance to handle our matters is that sometimes it just seems too complex and that it is going to take too dang long to double check the legal implications. I cannot argue with that. Asserting our rights, watching our back, and staying on our toes at all times can be exhausting.

Have you ever been buying something and you were presented with a contract or an agreement and started to read it but then you stopped? You started flipping through the pages to see how long that sucker was? After seeing it was over five pages of little fine print, your eyes glazed over and you just said, "F it!"…as in, *FORGET IT* and you just went ahead, said a prayer, crossed your fingers, and signed it. I must admit, I have even been there before.

You figure it is too long, the fine print is too small, and there was a lot of complicated legalese sprinkled throughout. Since you knew you wanted it and were going to buy it anyway, you rationalize that it is probably standard and trust everyone means you well. You figure it is just a small purchase. You figure, what is the worst that can happen anyway. And this is the very thinking that trips the rest of us up. The super wealthy know the devil is in the details and they have the legal resources to have help to cross their t's and dot their i's.

So, here is the hack:

It is not just the big-ticket legal issues that cause the biggest woes, it is the day-to-day life that piles up and affects our quality of life -death by a thousand cuts or compound effects.

Becoming legally savvy does not happen overnight. It is an accumulation of legally savvy disciplines over time that make a difference in your quality of life. I think the rest of us have more financial struggles because we encounter issues that in most cases are too small to hire an attorney in the traditional way, but big enough that it stings our pockets or wounds our pride. Throughout our lives we lose $50 here or $1,000 there. We get a speeding ticket fine here. Our home insurance company refuses to cover an air conditioning repair there. And, by the time we are middle aged we have over $100,000 lost out there and may be working a job just because we had to recover. Sadly, because the traditional way to access attorneys is out of budget for the rest of us in these small moments, it has become cheaper to be taken advantage of than to protect our rights. But, in the long run, it is not cheaper.

Rick was the manager at a swanky event hall. But his passion was baking. A few years back he opened a bakery downtown by the coast called Pie Seas Bakery since the store was beachfront, and it was his wife's birthday sign. He invested his life's savings to launch the bakery.

He needed a sign made and was approached by a vendor to design and install it. While Rick had used an attorney to help him set up his business as an LLC, he figured this was just an agreement for a sign. What was the worst that could happen? So he signed the agreement, contract unread and paid the first payment to get the sign going.

The sign technician started to install it but after a rainstorm when part of it was torn down he did not return to repair it. Rick called multiple times and each time the office said they would send someone. But, no one came.

Eventually Rick was fined $2,250 for having an unkempt sign according to the terms of his commercial lease. He got the fine and called the sign vendor to pay for it. They referred him to the signed contract that they would not be held liable for the building regulations. Rick felt stuck and eventually closed the bakery.

That small contract for a sign was the beginning of the end of Rick's dreams and he took the job at the event hall to recover his life's savings.

On the other hand:

There was a family who was getting an alarm installed in their home. Since it was a contract, they sent it to their attorney to review. They are glad they did. The attorney advised them that the contract was a five-year contract, notified them of their privacy expectations with respect to the security cameras being installed and the terms on how to break the lease if they needed to for any reason. The homeowners signed the contract well-informed and needed to break the agreement early because they got a job opportunity cross-country. They followed the procedures their attorney told them about and seamlessly were able to move on.

And one final example:

> *There was a freelance teacher who was offered a summer school job to teach a course at an academy. The academy had a contract for the teacher to sign. She was really excited about the opportunity and had a lot of respect for the school administrators. When she received the contract, she was tempted to just sign it and return it to the academy. But, she was legally savvy. She sent the contract to her attorney to review. The attorney was so glad she sent it to her and returned the contract all marked up in red with major areas to revise. One of the areas of the contract was information on how the teacher would be compensated. The attorney advised that the clause was way too vague and if a dispute arose would be extremely hard to challenge before a judge.*
>
> *The teacher appreciated the feedback and was able to get back to the academy and say "my attorney said" these areas need revision. The academy appreciated the feedback, made the revisions according to the teacher's request and she had a great time teaching that summer and was paid on time.*

I think it does not hurt for parties you are dealing with to know you are legally savvy and consult with attorneys.

The legally savvy get guidance on the "little things" as well as the big things. And as Coach John Wooden said, "If you don't have time to do it right, when do you have time to do it over?"

Legal questions pop up more often in life than we think. Every stage of life presents new questions and potential challenges. From birth, through school days, to falling in love, to starting a family, to aging, and passing away; thousands of laws come into play.

Have you ever thought this, or some variation of it?

- If I am buying a home with an HOA can I have that contract reviewed ahead of time, especially since I heard horror stories about others getting taken by their HOAs?
- Now that recreational marijuana is legal, can I light up at my job – just during break time?
- If I move my hair salon to my home and my client says I damaged her scalp, can she sue me for my house?
- If my cute new puppy is a biter or gets bitten by another dog at the dog park and now I have a sick dog and a veterinarian bill, who is responsible for paying for that?
- If my child is getting bullied at school and the school and the principal do not seem to care because it happened off campus, who do I need to talk to to stop the bullying?
- If I got an awesome opportunity to move to Istanbul and my landlord said it was cool for me to break my lease early, how can I be sure she won't come back and stick me for the remaining rent?
- If my shady spouse took my portion of the Covid-19 stimulus check can I get it back?
- If I'm writing my memoir to share my story and it includes me having to share my cousin's kooky and possibly incriminating role in it, will I get in trouble?
- If my cell phone company has still been charging me for a service I know I canceled months before, can I get that money back?
- If the city sends me a photo radar ticket for running a red light in the mail but the picture doesn't look like me, can I just ignore it?
- If I kept my end of the bargain and made this bride's wedding dress, but she is already back from her honeymoon and still hasn't paid me, how do I get my check?

What do all of these statements have in common? By now your legally savvy receptors should be firing off as you realize these are all legal issues!

The Covid-19 pandemic alone, revealed a host of major questions including the following scenario:

> *At the beginning of the Covid-19 pandemic there were four college roommates living together in an off-campus apartment. Their landlord posted a notice of eviction on their door.*
>
> *The college students were worried. Not only did they have to navigate their campus shutting down, staying quarantined, and figuring out how to run 4 zoom sessions simultaneously from their small apartment, they now had to deal with whether they would be homeless.*
>
> *One of the roommates vaguely heard about the moratorium on evictions but was not sure if it applied to their situation. Fortunately, one of the roommates had access to a law firm. She was able to call and speak with a landlord/ tenant attorney. That attorney was aware and up-to-date on the rapidly changing laws and was able to inform her that the moratorium did apply to them and to go back to the landlord and tell him the three most powerful words in the English language, "My attorney said" you cannot evict us because of the moratorium.*
>
> *The landlord stumbled over his words and acquiesced. The college students were able to remain in their apartment and ride out the pandemic.*

But, as we come out of the fog of the pandemic, new issues are arising. The eviction moratorium will eventually expire. The types of questions people have will be many. Do they have a duty to repay missed payments, can their landlord evict them, can they continue to work from home, and if there will be additional relief payouts for renters, among others?

Logical and Legal Solutions May Not be the Same

The law is not always logical. If it were, we would not need accredited law schools and highly regulated lawyers. There is a complexity often behind the seemingly simple. Just because something may sound like a logical solution does not mean it is close to a legal solution.

Say your boss does not pay you your last paycheck. But since you still have the key to his office you figure you will just hold the key as collateral until the boss pays you, almost like a ransom. Sounds logical right? Or, what if your apartment had a water leak your landlord has yet to fix. But now the rent is due so you rationalize that you will withhold the rent until the landlord fixes your plumbing. Sounds fair right? Or your soon to be ex-partner secretly drained your bank account leaving you embarrassed and asking for a handout from your parents. So, your BFF floats the idea of you posting those compromising pictures you had of her on social media. It is just poetic justice, right?

Wrong! In all these cases, your response would be in violation of law. From childhood, many of us were taught the adage that two wrongs do not make a right. But, on its face, these responses may not strike one as wrong. Well, maybe posting the embarrassing photographs screams shady to you. But, a lot of times, like in the examples above, it is not clear on how to properly handle a situation. You may have some heightened emotions firing off or friends in your ear telling you how they would have handled the issue *back in the day*. But perhaps that was another era or even another country.

Law is country, state, and time specific. At least every election cycle brings about changes in law and our state and federal legislatures are proposing changes as well. So, out of date advice can be some of the worst advice too. And for the rest of us, we have not had a lot of experience on how to be legally savvy when handling life's situations. We did not have the opportunity to be coached and guided by attorneys as we grew up. We need to build up the practice. For advice on how to handle disputes, you want to consult with an attorney.

Consulting with an attorney will also help you to know what you are dealing with. There are some people who make their own rules that cover their ideal scenarios. It is important to be able to discern if it is law or just someone's policy.

OR, if it is the elevated stupidity a recent GQ magazine op-ed interpreted . This is happening a lot. There are some people who sound so convincing, but they are utterly wrong. *One woman went to check on one of her accounts at the bank and when the teller found out she was married encouraged her to add her spouse to the account.* But this was horrible advice. The teller just converted her separate property into community property!

The legally savvy get guidance on how to discern these issues. They know doing it sooner is better. The legally savvy see legal advice not as a last resort, but as a regular course of life. They know the small things are what can have a major impact on your life.

It Wasn't Me – Identity Theft is a Legal Issue

Fraud around all types of benefits including employment, unemployment, stimulus relief, and disability benefits have been hard hit. Romance scams, recreational car purchases, and more persist.

Identity theft has been a major issue and it has been exacerbated by the pandemic. The legally savvy are mindful of this. They know that an incident of identity theft can be just a small tip of a ginormous iceberg and often has a legal remedy to it.

Identity theft is perpetrated by people of all backgrounds and upon people of all walks of life – the young, the elder, foreign, the domestic, the rich, and the poor.

- A woman's bank account was shorted thousands of dollars after a bank employee stole her account info and sold it on the dark web.

- A college student was denied a student loan because he already had one in his name. However, it was not him! His personal information was stolen by a fast food employee from his job a few summers before to sell in an identity theft racket.

- A Colorado man made homeless by the economic crisis was wrongly disqualified from receiving public assistance. Colorado's agency's report showed him working a full-time job in Washington state. Someone stole his identity to work while simultaneously receiving disability benefits in his own name.

- A 70-year-old woman while dying in her nursing home was robbed of thousands of dollars by a man who gained access to her accounts. He struck her 84-year-old neighbor as well.

- An Arizona man received notice from his bank that an email request was made to wire transfer $83,000 from his account to buy a Chevrolet Camaro for his brother-in-law. When asked by the bank clerk to verify that email, he did not. It turned out a man in Boston was buying the car and had been siphoning off money from the Scottdale man's account for months. He was stuck paying for a car bill for a car he never saw. He did not get assistance in time to help him prove that he never purchased that car. But, to prevent his credit score from plummeting he paid the bill anyway.

- Sadly, we often learn that we were preyed upon by someone close to us. A man found out he lost $10,000 after his ex-wife fraudulently opened a bank account in his name three years after they divorced. She still had his social security number, date of birth and other personal data.

- A disbarred lawyer used his smarts and charm to con a woman he met on an online site to date him. He lied about most of the information about himself. According to the Department of Justice release he "lied about his age, his educational background, his family's wealth, and failed to disclose his prior federal conviction for fraud." He eventually moved in with her, gained access to her personally identifying information, and went to town opening accounts in her name and using those accounts to pay for his own plastic surgery.

While the financial havoc identity thieves wreak is a mess, many find out they are a victim of identity theft when they are arrested by police.

- Guzman has been arrested multiple times and has spent weeks and months in jail at a time. His identity was stolen. Each time it gets cleared up but the legal system is slow and it took up to one month to see the fingerprints did not match and release him.
- Monica, in Columbus, GA was arrested for failing to appear for a traffic ticket she had no idea she received. Her roommate was stopped by the police twice within a few days and each time the roommate provided Monica's information. Monica had no idea the person bailing her out of jail was the one who got her in there.
- Sandra was an elementary school teacher. Police walked into her classroom and arrested her while she was teaching. There was a warrant for her arrest for prostitution except it was not her! Someone bought her identity and gave it to the police when she was arrested.

Being legally savvy about identity theft is key to preventing it from becoming a disaster. In some cases, it is simply calling up the bank and asking them to cancel a fraudulent withdrawal. But, more often than not you may need an attorney to prevent you from being arrested for someone else's actions or for them to send a letter for you explaining your innocence. Remember, the little things matter too.

Legally Savvy Hacks

The Legally Savvy know…

- ✓ The devil is in the details.
- ✓ To ask an attorney to discern whether something is law or just someone's policy.
- ✓ To protect their identity.

I must undertake to love myself and to respect myself and to respect myself as though my very life depends upon self-love and self-respect.

— Maya Angelou

CHAPTER 7

Legally Savvy in Love

What's love got to do with it?

— Tina Turner

ove is complex. It is fun, romantic, and sweet. But, when love is in the air, it is a good time to apply a legal 'air' filter. Legally speaking, issues relating to family life can be costly and stressful. Year after year, we find family issues are one of the top 5 areas where people seek out lawyers for help. I have heard attorneys say they are simply fine with people having these challenges because if people were savvier about these areas of life they would be out of a job. Most attorneys' business model is such that their income, unfortunately, is derived from untangling your messes. I am free from relying on that business model and I would rather not see people unnecessarily suffer.

Being more legally savvy when it comes to our family, especially the family we choose, is critical and can save us money and so much more.

Daytime television ratings are high for salacious shows like Maury, where people tune in to find out "who the baby daddy is." Those episodes may seem comical and over the top, but issues of paternity pop up more often than you think in regular families who may live next door or work in the office next to you.

Life can get legal quickly and you want to be legally savvy about your personal life. Again, being legally savvy is not a license to be a jerk or manipulative. In fact, it is a critical form of self-care, wellness, and setting healthy boundaries.

Married or not, many of us just do not realize all the legal ramifications that are triggered when we get into a relationship. Most of us were not taught about all the legalities that arise when that relationship may turn into marriage or if that relationship produces children.

Falling in Love

Falling in love and getting married can be one of the most blissful times of your life. Every girl dreams of being a princess on her wedding day. Every guy dreams about the wedding night. Falling in love can be an incredible experience. Yet, because it is so intimate, it can also be the gateway to some of the worst pain you could ever know.

Often in dating or courting for marriage the conversations that are had lack depth. People get lured by superficial facts like sharing the same taste in music, being fans of the same basketball team, and let us be real, just sharing the same ethnicity. These add flavor to a relationship, but in and of themselves are not factors that make a long-term marital relationship work.

It is better to find out whether you are or are not on the same page with a potential partner as far as goals, beliefs, values, and communication style beforehand rather than after you pay those thousands of dollars on the deposit for your wedding venue, for the rings and wedding dress. I would not want you to be that person paying for a divorce on top of still paying off your wedding! I have seen this and it is not fun. I have also seen where a person cannot afford a divorce because they are still paying off their wedding, so they are in a toxic situation from which they cannot get out. The saying "love is grand, but divorce is ten grand" bears some serious truth! I hate to break it to you but divorces can be and often are more than ten grand. So, talk it out – ahead of time! Invest in yourself and take the time to do your part in seeing if this relationship is a healthy fit for you or not.

Most attorneys are not going to tell you this because most people are not going to go to them early. Unfortunately, most people are not prevention minded anyway. Most people operate from the mentality that "if it ain't broke then don't try to fix it" thinking that if they bring up an uncomfortable subject it may push the person they have decided they wanted away. People's confirmation bias kicks in way too fast before they know who a person is. That means that they have decided this person is right for them and choose not to hear or will tune their ear to only hear things that confirm this person is the one. Confirmation bias is a sly cognitive trick many can fall susceptible too.

I know many of us grew up with the principle that generally all people are good. Well, as you embark on the journey of love and partnership, I hate to break it to you, but that is not true. It is important to understand that all people are not good. There are wolves in sheep's clothing amongst the kind and empathetic ones. And, as long as we continue to live in the dark about the fact that there are wolves in sheep's clothing and fail to take the necessary steps to protect ourselves, we will continue to be taken advantage of, hoodwinked, and duped.

I know this sounds cynical. Some of you may have been expecting to hear all about satin ribbons and butterflies in the chapter on love. That is not this book. This book is about arming you with the mindset to masterfully navigate life.

It is naive to think that everyone has your best interest at heart. You do not know what another person is thinking. You are not a mind reader. No, everyone is not out to get you either. But it is important to not project your ethics and positivity onto everyone you meet. Just because you would not renege on your word does not mean someone else would not. Some people were raised that it is okay to step on others to get what they want. There are people who would rejoice if you suffered.

> *A Quranic injunction says there are people who "if a good befalls you, it grieves them, but if some evil overtakes you, they rejoice at it." -Quran Chapter 3, Verse 120*
>   *This was revealed over 1400 years ago. So don't be deluded.*

Others have been taught that we attract what we are. But that is not necessarily true. Sometimes we attract what someone wants from us: our looks, status, money, or even family name. Their intentions may be wholesome, but then again they may not. Sincere people and con artists both look alike; in the beginning. It turns out we are not as great judges of people as we think we are. Since you do not know who is who yet it is a good idea to vet that out before jumping head first into the deep end of love.

So here is the hack:

- Remember, everyone does not operate from the same value system as you do.

Some people are not good. Some people lie. There are people who do not have good intentions. There are people who have narcissistic or sociopathic personality disorders where they may exploit you without a conscience. Those kinds of people do not target dumb people. They target people with soft hearts and empathy from all educational levels because they can count on you sacrificing yourself for them. But they had no intentions, despite what they said, to reciprocate the sacrifice. If you stop and think, you may have encountered someone like this before from your family of origin, a friend, a prior romantic partner, or boss who never seemed to take their turn sacrificing. They may have sacrificed if it made them look good in front of others or if it had a simultaneous benefit to them. But it was short lived and insincere.

Other red flags exist to help you spot toxic, narcissistic people, and liars. A big tip off is if they push over your boundaries as it pertains to your finances, time, or anywhere you set a boundary. It is worth it spending some time learning about the patterns of abusers and controllers to help yourself avoid them. You want to avoid altogether making contracts, especially in a marriage contract with these kinds of people. Count on them to be vindictive, conniving, and as manipulative of the legal system as they have been of you.

Equally important to remember is that there are some people who are underdeveloped in some areas. They may not be able to regulate their emotions maturely. They could stand to engage in some additional personal development. They may be kind but highly irresponsible with their money. They may be good savers but clueless about how to run a home. The legally savvy understand not everyone is as conscientious as they are and plan accordingly. You want to at least minimize your risks as much as possible if personally binding yourself with these folks.

Getting Married

This aspect of life is not taken as seriously as it should be despite prevailing information out there:

- From religious texts we learn minding our associations, especially our closest ones, is paramount.

- In leading books on business and career, warnings are made about choosing a partner who is supportive of and shares your wealth goals because a healthy marriage can build you up financially or bankrupt you.

Social science research reveals that healthy marriages help people stay healthier all around and to live longer.

Wake Forest University psychologists found that marriage does more to promote life satisfaction than money, sex, or even children. In fact, men's health fares the best in healthy marriages. The same studies also revealed that unhealthy relationships can wreak havoc on your physical and mental health.

My mother and marriage preparation pioneer would lament that people "plan more for the wedding than they do the marriage." The rates of divorce and child custody cases that my colleagues and I see bear this truth out. People meticulously plan out the details of the wedding reception's seating arrangement more than they plan out where they are going to live after marriage, who pays for what, and if a conflict arises, how they will address it! They figure that will just work itself out despite knowing that issues around money account for one of the top reasons couples head toward divorce!

One hack to remember in dealing with the legalities of life is that it is far better to stay out of trouble than to try to get out of trouble. Before permanently coupling or going down the wedding aisle, there are some legally savvy conversations that you will want to have with yourself first and then your partner to avoid catastrophes. That is why I would advise you, along with marriage counseling or a marriage preparation class, to go through each one of the following areas with your potential partner.

- Confirmation of Marital Status
- Civil or Religious Ceremony, or Both
- Religious Contracts
- Financial Values

- Marriage, Money and the Law Where You Live
- Pre- and/or Post-Nuptial Agreements
- Marriage and Immigration Status
- Criminal History

I would also advise you to consult with a family law attorney prior to deciding to get married.

Confirmation of Marital Status

The first legally savvy question to ask a potential partner is a big one. I am not sure you are ready for this but here goes. The question to ask is:

- Are you married?

I know. I know! This seems like it should be obvious, but in this day and age, my friends, presume nothing! As we discussed earlier, some people just straight up lie about their marital status. For others, marital status is complicated.

- There are some people who have filed for divorce but are still in the midst of proceedings. Divorce does not happen overnight. It can take months, and in some cases, a few years to finalize the divorce. Some states have a minimum amount of time they require couples to go through before they can get divorced.
- In other cases, there are complex issues of how to divide assets and debts and child custody matters that take time, especially when they are dealing with an antagonistic soon-to-be ex.
- There may be a scenario no one could foresee like a global health pandemic like Covid-19 or Hurricane Katrina that devastates entire states and creates delays in already backed up court systems. There are people today dealing with the aftermath of these tragedies.

- There are some people who had intentions to get a divorce, but because money was tight, they just never got around to it and forgot all about it.
- There are others who had a difficult spouse and wanted to just get away. Others still had situations where they had children and did not want to jeopardize losing their children by setting off the other spouse by filing for a divorce.
- Lots of people check out of their marriage emotionally and even physically way before it legally ends. So, some may say they are divorced when in actuality they are only divorced in their minds. Others perhaps went through a religious divorce so they consider themselves sufficiently divorced because they claim God is the most important one it matters to anyway. This is a laudable idea, but irresponsible and is legally incorrect. I think we can agree God is not a fan of Team Irresponsible!
- Some are still holding out hope that their marriage will be reconciled so they are just biding their time and not getting divorced.
- Some are trying to make their spouse jealous by being with you.
- And let us be real, some are just playing the field. There are people who go on in these types of arrangements for years and even decades.

So, if you go on some of the dating or matrimonial match-making sites, do not assume that everyone on there is officially, as Pitbull says, single and ready to mingle. But, you will want to do some research either way. If the potential spouse said they were married before, ask to see the divorce documents or try to look them up on your own through their state superior court's website or on the court's websites where they said they lived. If you can, it would not hurt to look up everywhere they said they lived. This is harder to verify when your potential partner comes from another country, especially if you are not an expert of that country, so beware!

Unless you are dealing with your best friend who you grew up with since childhood and never had gaps in hanging out, it is wise to presume you do not know them well enough and should do more than just take their word. You will want some receipts! You can ask in a playful way, such as "show me yours and I'll show you mine." But get clarity on this issue, lest it comes back to bite you.

> There was a woman, Raquel, married to a man for 25 years. She was committed and saw her husband through a serious illness that eventually proved fatal. After she laid him to rest, she collected herself to settle all the remaining affairs. One of those was to collect her husband's social security payouts to continue to afford to live in her home. Well, it turns out he was never divorced from his first wife so Raquel's marriage was not recognized. The first wife collected the social security and did not share a dime with Racquel.

Additionally, and let us be adults here, estranged spouses have reconciled for either a one-night stand or permanently. If they are not divorced, the door is still open to rekindle that relationship. They have history together so it is not far-fetched that that history can continue to pull them together and if you have already made agreements with this person you could be stuck. Say you rented an apartment together or bought a car. Say you left a business for them or your job. You will have some legal questions to work through if you claim you want to break the lease on the apartment because your girl is going back to her husband. Or you want your job back because he will not support you because his earnings are now garnished for more child support. To avoid any confusion, I advise people to close one door before peeping into another.

Civil or Religious Ceremony, or Both

For various reasons some people prefer to live together without having an official marriage license. Some people are more secular and decline the formal marriage route. Others may have a religious draw to getting married but would rather not get married civilly. Perhaps the other spouse has major debt they want to keep away from impacting their spouse. Or there are some who are younger and their finances are too limited to have their dream wedding, so they prefer to live together while they save but still keep it "right with God."

- You will want to consider if you will have a civil marriage ceremony, just a religious ceremony, or both?

In the United States, except under some strict circumstances such as in Texas, you are only legally married if you are civilly married. That means that you and your partner took a trip to the courthouse together, showed your identification cards to the clerk of the court, and paid for a marriage license. That marriage license must be properly officiated and signed by the parties or officiant depending on the state's requirements and witnessed at the ceremony. Some religious institutions and leaders only agree to officiate a religious marriage if it is done simultaneously with a civil marriage. Some pastors, imams, and rabbis have caught wind of how some people have attempted to manipulate an unsuspecting partner by not getting married according to the state law.

I caution people to not go down the road of opting for just a religious ceremony because their fiancé is still technically married to someone else. That is a precarious situation. In terms of the current spouse, upon civil marriage, certain rights and responsibilities would have been triggered. Default inheritance laws and rights to government benefits like social security kicked in. Default power of attorney rights over medical decisions kicked in. The rest of us have not been leaders in getting wills and powers of attorneys in place. So, if you religiously marry someone who is still civilly married to someone else you may be in for a rude awakening about what you can do and what their current spouse still has rights to do.

Religious Contracts

The United States is a country that has embedded in it the principle of separation of church and state. It also protects the free exercise of religion in the first amendment of the U.S. Constitution. So, if you ascribe to a religious tradition in this country, you have the right to freely practice your religion. These two principles together mean that while you are free to enter into the agreement as part of practicing your faith, the state will not enforce that religious agreement because it does not involve itself in matters of internal religious interpretation or enforcement. This means that if you ascribe to a minority religion, getting your practices enforced can be a separate challenge.

If you think about it, each follower can have their own interpretation of which religious practice is more authentically Christian, Hindu, Jewish or Islamic. Could you imagine a Judge, unfamiliar with the depth and breadth of your tradition, making an interpretation as to what is orthodox or not?

This issue came to a head in the family law case of Victor v. Victor out of Arizona that basically says a court will not get involved in religious matters. The wife in the case asserted that she would be in limbo, if she does not obtain a *gett*, an official divorce in orthodox Jewish law that the husband has to agree to. The husband was not going to do it and basically told the court, nanny nanny boo boo, you can't make me! The court agreed with him.

In-Depth Case Study – Jewish Divorce

Perri and Warren Victor got married in an orthodox Jewish ceremony in Florida. As part of their marriage and in accordance with Jewish law, they "entered into" a ketubah. This is a document recording the financial obligations that the husband undertakes toward his wife in respect of, and consequent to, their marriage--obligations that, in principle, are imposed on him by Jewish law." The ketubah provides in part that the parties will comply with the "laws of Moses and Israel" and that a husband will fulfill his obligations to cherish, honor, and support his wife in accordance with those laws.

In this case, the ketubah was a general, standardized document without any provisions tailored to these parties. Both parties signed the ketubah, but it was not acknowledged as required at the time (This is no longer required in Arizona).

Mrs. Victor sought to have the court enforce the ketubah as a prenuptial agreement to require Mr. Victor to properly go about a Jewish divorce as well. Mrs. Victor attested that even if she has a civil divorce, without a proper Jewish divorce she would still religiously be married and unable to remarry. Any children she had if she was not properly divorced from Warren would be considered illegitimate.

Mr. Victor asserted that the court could not compel him to follow a religious practice and that the ketubah lacked formality sufficient to consider it an enforceable prenuptial agreement. Mrs. Victor argued that she was not asking the court to order Mr. Victor to practice a religious act, but rather to compel him to do what he said he would do.

But, the court agreed with Mr. Victor. The court will not enter into the jurisdiction of interpreting religion. It cannot compel someone to engage in a religious act. And, the ketubah was not completed with the proper formality to be considered a valid prenuptial agreement. Stating compliance "with the law of Moses and Israel" was too vague to enforce.

Muslim women also find themselves in this type of limbo all the time. Since we do not have Shariah courts in the U.S. I have seen Muslim marriages encounter almost the exact same issues. At their marriage ceremonies in accordance with Islamic law, they typically sign a one-page *nikah*. The nikah, a religiously binding marriage agreement, often sites language such as "this marriage will comply with the rulings of Allah and the Messenger Muhammad (peace be upon him)." Typically, the nikah does not explicitly say how one would go about a divorce if the marriage did not work, which religious center or masjid board would preside over it, or whose property is whose and how it would be divided.

These aspects of the religious contracts may be pre-written into the law in Israel for the Jewish community or the Islamic requirements in countries that have a majority Muslim population, but not in America. Observant followers of minority faiths here have been plagued over these issues and often find themselves in a precarious limbo. They may wonder whether, despite finalizing a divorce in the U.S. court, they are actually free to move on. They may have presumed that because their spouse signed on to the religious mandate for spousal maintenance and support they would have nothing to worry about. There are no shariah courts in the U.S. that can enforce an Islamic nikah.

Sadly, in the U.S., no matter how shameful one spouse's behavior is, the secular courts can not step in and provide relief outside of its jurisdiction and the religious courts have no authority. Most minority religious communities in the U.S. do not have enforcement mechanisms, maybe outside of community shaming, which I am not opposed to, to compel a person to follow the wholesome guidance of the religion.

So, if the observance of your faith or values are important to you, choose wisely as to whom you marry. Your marriage will only be as good as the two of you make it. This is why I encourage us, especially those who follow minority community faiths, to be more legally savvy about how we can realistically handle our religious observances under secular civil law.

The other thing you can do is use the legal tools within the United States that give you the opportunity to have a formal and enforceable premarital agreement. So, you may still have a ketubah or a nikah that may still be considered highly valuable to you spiritually. But, then you should also enter into a prenuptial agreement with specificities about what you and your partner agree to be bound to.

You could incorporate some of the principles of the nikah or ketubah by specifically spelling out in a prenuptial agreement what those principles are that the parties are agreeing to be bound by. So instead of saying 'the husband agrees to support his wife under Jewish law,' you would specifically lay out what that support would look like – with percentages, dollar amounts, and more. Semantically, a prenuptial agreement is not a religious contract, but its content can be a contract that is aligned with your religious values. See the difference? That way, it can actually be enforceable by a secular U.S. court.

Many of the issues and principles above can also be extrapolated to apply to other minority or non-majority family structures.

Financial Values

Discussing how a person handles money, debts, or if they have any outstanding tax issues is important to know about. It could be a minor issue to handle or it could be catastrophic. Do not sweep these conversations under the rug or wait until after the wedding. The only surprises you want after you are married is that the person is even nicer than you thought they were or they are taking you to Jamaica for your birthday!

Remember that the legally savvy do their best to also be financially savvy and always have some income to their name. I'm not saying it should be secretive. But, you do not want to be destitute if you can help it. It is those environments that leave people ripe for abuse.

Marriage, Money, and the Law Where You Live

You want to know the marital property system you plan to get married under, live under, or move to. As far as property, each state in the United States is designated as either a community property state or a separate property state also known as a common law state. If you get married, this will determine a great deal about how assets and liabilities are shared absent any other marital agreements.

While the community property states have rules that they share, be mindful that they do have their uniqueness. The same thing goes for the common law states. Look at the state in which you reside and know which type of marital property state it is.

The 9 community property law states are Arizona, California, Idaho, Louisiana, Nevada, New Mexico, Texas, Washington, Wisconsin and the Commonwealth of Puerto Rico. The rest of the states are common law states. Let us look at Arizona and Michigan to illustrate a bit of how these different legal approaches work.

Arizona is a community property state. What that means is any property that you acquired prior to marriage is your separate property. However, what is acquired during the course of the marriage, unless it was given to you as a gift or you inherited it, is presumed that of the community (marital partnership). That means that whatever earnings are made during the marriage by either spouse is equally owned by each of the spouses. It does not matter if one spouse was the sole breadwinner in the family. That also means any liabilities like debts will also be shared. So, for example, the home you purchase during the marriage is shared. If one spouse has a gambling addiction and racks up a lot of debt during the marriage the marital union is held liable for that too.

You should ensure that you are clear on how the property laws work where you live or you may inadvertently give a former partner access to your assets that you do not want them to have if you separate or divorce.

I cringe when I hear, usually women, say they plan to marry rich so they do not have to worry about money. Unfortunately, when that happens, they may give up or feel pressured to stay out of the financial affairs of the house. It is important to remember that a future spouse may not do you right financially, they may not be just, so you do not want to give away your rights or agency as a newlywed. You do not know them, you do not know if you can trust them.

Even when dealing with your longer-term spouse, do not sign forms if you do not know what they are. People have been unwittingly locked out of major decisions or given up their just claim to certain property. There was a woman in Missouri whose husband sold their house right from under her nose. He would have only been able to do that if she provided some kind of written consent and she does not remember signing anything.

If you do have income from before you get married that is classified as your separate property. However, you may commingle your funds with that of the community. If the marriage goes downhill, this can be immensely problematic. If you had separate property and you relinquished your separate property right by using community funds to repair the house, for example and the marriage goes sour, now the soon to be ex-partner is entitled to their share of that property because it was not treated as separate during the marriage.

Take for example Moira.

> *While Moira was single, she inherited a slice of a farm in California that had been in her family since the 1800s. Her cousins who lived on the other plots of the farm cared for her portion as well. They would sell the eggs and milk from the farm at the local farmer's market and send Moira the profits.*
>
> *A year later, Moira met Mike and he talked about his love of farming. A year after that, they were married at a ceremony on the farm. One week after they returned from their honeymoon, Moira added Mike's name to the deed of the farm. She figured they could sell the eggs and milk together at the farmer's market.*
>
> *Fifteen years and two children later, Moira filed for divorce from Mike. His hidden alcoholism had come out and she just could not take it anymore. She listed the inherited farm as her separate property.*

> *Mike countered and said that it was community property as his name was on the deed and he helped to farm the land and helped run the business of selling the goods. The proceeds, he said, they lived on. The court agreed with Mike that Moira's separate property had been converted to community property. Moira was not able to afford to buy Mike out and so they had to sell the land and split the profit from the sale down the middle.*
>
> *Moira was livid as her cousins were too. They now had strangers as neighbors on the family farm.*

Consider on the other hand a professional basketball player, Doc.

> *Doc played internationally and earned bonuses when his team won several championships. Doc had saved up one million dollars in his account. When Doc returned to Arizona, he and his fiancé, Fatima got married. Fatima gave up her job in the media.*
>
> *A week after the wedding, Doc withdrew $500,000 from the account and bought a swanky vacation home in Denver. Doc and Fatima would spend long weekends and summers in the vacation home. Any time maintenance was required on this home, Doc would dip into his earnings from his past bonuses, until they separated and eventually filed for divorce ten years later. Doc listed the home as his sole and separate property.*
>
> *His wife countered and claimed that since it was purchased during marriage it was presumptively community property and should be divided in half. The court agreed with Doc. Doc had kept good records and could trace and show with clear and convincing evidence that the house was purchased and maintained with his sole and separate property.*

And finally, red flags popped up for one young woman, Laila.

Laila had property given to her when she graduated college as was her family tradition. A few years later she was introduced to Ismael who seemed like he was smart, sweet, well off, and from a good family. They eventually got married.

The very next day Ismael asked Laila about adding his name to her property. She was taken off guard by the question but did not take it seriously. As the year went on, Ismael became more aggressive about having his name added to her property. He became aggressive in other areas as well.

Laila refused and never asked Ismael to help her pay taxes or maintain the property. But, once she had their first child she stopped working. Ismael flat out declined to help her maintain her properties unless his name was on it. So instead, Laila's family helped her with the properties.

The relationship between Laila and Ismael worsened. He was relentlessly heaping narcissistic psychological and physical abuse on Laila and she filed for divorce.

In the divorce, Ismael claimed again that Laila's property was half his. Fortunately Laila had an attorney who was able to help her gather what was needed to prove the properties had never changed to community property and were still her separate property.

That was not the only battle Laila had to fight with Ismael. It usually is not in these cases.

In Arizona, as discussed above, community property is the default marital property arrangement. In common law states, such as Michigan for example, common law is the default marital property arrangement. All in all, that means that the state has a plan for you if you do not have one.

Some people do not work or have an additional independent source of income when they get married. Historically, this has been the case for some women but it can also be for men. They may opt out of working to support their spouse and the children. And so what winds up happening is they do not have their own independent money which means that, if needed, often they may not be able to afford to access an attorney to check on their rights. This may be something that you wish to consider addressing directly in a prenuptial agreement.

Pre- and/or Post-Nuptial Agreements

You can create another arrangement you and your spouse prefer to follow by entering into a prenuptial or post-nuptial agreement. Prenuptial agreements, agreements before the marriage, have been given a bad reputation. It seemed like it was just for rich men to keep their lower-income wives away from their money. But ethically managed, they are great tools under a lot more circumstances.

Those who have religious beliefs around money and marriage have a fantastic tool with the prenuptial agreement. For example, in Islam, women are not obligated to share their earnings that they acquired from salary, business profits, or inheritance with anyone. It is hers to save, use, or invest as she pleases. It is the husband's responsibility to financially provide for the needs of the family. So, a prenuptial agreement could be drafted to opt out of the community property plan that would retain this scenario.

A prenuptial agreement, in essence, is a great financial management tool. It allows the couple to bypass the divorce rules of their state and provides you a prime opportunity to discuss expectations for your marriage.

Pretty much anything can be written in the prenuptial agreement (with some exceptions discussed below). The most common clauses set out who would own what property and how it would be distributed in the event of a divorce.

I know, it is not at first glance, the most romantic discussion. However, discussing this is a good opportunity to gauge how you and your boo would handle other conversations about finances in your marriage. For some couples a prenuptial agreement can bring them closer. It is a good opportunity to discuss your expectations about marriage, money, and other serious questions you would want to have settled prior to getting married. If this conversation goes well, it is a good sign. If it does not, well, that is a sign too.

In your conversation and in the drafting, there are several factors to consider in putting a proper prenuptial agreement in place.

- Each party should have the agreement reviewed by their own separate attorney. This allows both parties to get fair advice as they do not necessarily have the same interests under the agreement. This makes sure that the attorney does not have a conflict of interest which can arise when both parties to an agreement are clients.

- There should be a reasonable distance between the drafting, review, and signing of the prenuptial agreement and the actual marriage. This timing allows both parties to have the capacity to get the appropriate advice and consider any changes that may be needed without being under duress to sign because of the date. Many attorneys will not even agree to assist with a prenup if the marriage date is less than one month away.

- Do not include clauses that are contrary to public policy. In America, for example, it could not say that the husband has the right to marry more than one wife. This may be permitted under Islamic law but in the U.S. it is a crime, and American laws apply (see previous discussion of the separation of church and state).

- In addition, any clauses in the prenuptial agreement that would result in a spouse being on public assistance are not allowed.

- Do not include any agreements about child custody. All child custody matters are determined under the relevant legislation of the jurisdiction where custody is being determined.

Finally, you do want to keep a copy in a safe place. My advice is to get a copy to a trusted friend or family member as soon as you execute it. I know someone who is pretty sure the husband conveniently "lost" the prenuptial agreement to attempt to get out of it.

Marriage and Immigration Status

Despite the accessibility of technology, long distance relationships can be quite emotionally and financially taxing - especially if they cross an ocean. Purchasing international plane tickets abroad every 4 to 6 months, sustaining two homes on different continents, and lonely nights can wear even the most optimistic person down.

The super wealthy also have an advantage here. I am curious to see how Megan and Prince Harry will be managing it now that they live in the U.S. But at least they have the best resources at their disposal. For those not so wealthy and famous, the immigration system in the United States leaves room to be desired. Similar to other systems in this country, in some ways it is good and in other ways it is disastrous. Many advocates and objectors would argue the immigration system is broken. It is not a balanced process.

When entertaining an international marriage there are legalities to be aware of. You need to know your potential partner's legal status in the United States. Is he or she a U.S. citizen? If not, does the person you want to marry have documentation to legally be here, is he or she a permanent resident, or will he or she require sponsorship to remain in the country.

You also want to be mindful that the immigration process could take years to complete. Similar to the Department of Motor Vehicle (DMV) or the Internal Revenue Services (IRS)of the U.S. Citizenship and Immigration Services (USCIS), the agency that processes visas and green cards, is not the easiest line to get through. You may find yourself frustrated trying to get help. They are backlogged and coming out of the pandemic does not make it any better.

If you meet someone inside the United States you will likely have to ask, if they do not offer up the information. If you meet someone abroad, you want to ask what their nationality is, their status with their country and their status with the U.S. This discussion is not about discrimmination, which I do not support. Rather, it is about understanding the legalities and how immigration affects your marriage. Some people have been barred from coming to the United States because of reasons outside of their control or they have already attempted to do so fraudulently. And citizens of some countries are more favored to enter the country than others.

There is no shade as to what that status is. The world has become more and more global in nature. People from all corners of the globe live in other countries including the United States. Technological advancements have made reaching out and meeting someone in another continent as easy as meeting someone up the street. Gone are the days when you had to go to a corner-market, buy a calling card, load it with money, and dial a super long number to connect for an expensive dollar a minute! Now, you can simply call someone for free through Facebook or WhatsApp. So, the thought of having a relationship with someone from another country can cross your mind.

Do not assume that just because someone is from another country that they are not a U.S. citizen. So, just have a conversation. You should just know because this will impact your life. Immigration policies change. Borders close. Borders reopen. Today, U.S. citizens do not need any extra visa or permission to pop in and out of many countries. Certain airports have swift service for people from certain countries while others are frequently pulled into "special rooms" for questioning. Unfortunately, it is not all fair. But, we already discussed earlier how privilege plays a part in these systems. While activists, attorneys, and informed legislators are working to bring more progress, the legally savvy do their best to manage what comes up in their life.

You will also want to know if you are entertaining a relationship with someone who is in the middle of removal proceedings and on the brink of being removed from the U.S. These cases can take months or even years before a person must actually get on an airplane. So, it may not be readily apparent without a conversation. Of course, use sensitivity perhaps by first asking about family origin, places their family lives, places they've lived, or traveled too, and if they plan to return for visits or to retire there. Just like whether someone is not quite divorced yet, the aspects of status can have major legal impacts for you. This could be a traumatizing situation if you thought you were going to have a long happy life together in the United States but your spouse is forced to leave. In your heart you may want to follow them wherever they go, but that may just not be practical.

- You may have your career established here and it would be near impossible to restart it in another country.
- You may already have children that you cannot uproot from their school or from their other parent.
- You may have elderly parents that need your support.
- You may be social and not know the language of your beloved's country. That may feel isolating and depressing if you cannot communicate as readily as you used too.

The lifestyle in the other country may not be to your tastes. A month backpacking abroad, using squatty potties, biking all around town, and siestas shutting down business in the middle of the day may be a great vacation, but may not be something you want to live with long term. Perhaps it is, but, being thrust into that situation and not having the chance to get acclimated could be a major turn off even if you love that person and feel safe with them.

- For professions that require licenses such as therapists, lawyers, and doctors, you may have to start from the very beginning with schooling to be able to work in that field abroad.

In terms of marriages, sadly, there are United States citizens who take advantage of immigrant spouses. There are immigrant spouses who take advantage of their citizen spouses. There are not enough checks and balances on both sides in my opinion. The system is impaired and, because it is, it permits enough ill-intended people to slip through which can leave the innocent people vulnerable whether they are immigrants or citizens. The legally savvy person is aware of this possibility and addresses these issues head on.

If you are a United States Citizen or a permanent resident and are eligible to sponsor a partner to come to the United States, be aware and do your due diligence to see if that is something you would want to do. You will want to know if the potential partner is who they say they are and you want to have deep knowledge of the other country and culture. Then give it time to help you accurately assess if this person genuinely wants to marry you and not that they just want to "marry America" as one astute uncle-type quipped.

International love can be a beautiful thing. It is a beautiful miracle to find someone who holds your same values, ethics, and shares a similar lifestyle even though you grew up a world apart. But, be legally savvy in this arena. Most people are not aware of a unique aspect of immigration law that makes it extra risky for U.S. citizens, so I want to be very clear. Be very aware that when sponsoring a person for marriage, the sponsor is financially responsible for that person FOR TEN YEARS, unless their visa is revoked, they have worked an equivalent of ten years, they leave the country permanently, they die, or become a citizen. This financial responsibility remains in effect WHETHER YOU ARE STILL MARRIED OR NOT. That means that even if you get divorced you are still obligated by federal law for them financially FOR TEN YEARS. So, if your international spouse is not able to support themselves or need public assistance you can potentially be sued to provide that financial assistance and ordered to provide it. Imagine divorcing a person you can't stand in your 20's but still being attached to that person in your 30's! One woman who went through this said she felt like she had a boulder to carry for ten years. Furthermore, say you need additional backup to sponsor your spouse such as your parents or a close friend, because you don't meet the financial threshold, they too are responsible for TEN YEARS. Yikes!

In essence, all of the financial risk is passed on to the U.S. Citizen sponsor. Most business people would say that is a bad deal. This is further complicated because there is little help for U.S. citizens who find out their marriage is not what they bargained for. Most people find out their international spouse was playing them for a green card shortly after they get it. They start pulling away, acting disinterested, cheating, or just plain disappearing. The sponsoring spouse hits a series of brick walls. Most immigration attorneys focus on bringing couples together not the aftermath if there is a breakup. So they find no help there. The visa and green card issuing agencies cater their services to the immigrant and not the sponsoring spouse. There is no formal process to revoke sponsorship. There is not a process in place where the sponsoring spouse can just have an appointment to get help. I have seen too many sponsoring spouses endure the stress of a divorce, the extra layer of mental strain from being betrayed, the exhaustion of not having anyone to turn to, and the burden they feel to carry this financial obligation looming over their heads. These are citizens who even have ties to the other country from where their spouse immigrated so presumably had more insight into the person they married and they still had problems.

Because of the frequency of green card marriage scams and this one-sided ten year financial obligation, I do not advise them. I highly recommend that if the person you love can lawfully find their own way to the United States, the better. A fellow attorney who handles the wreckage of these marriages has reached the point where she is opposed to bringing anyone into the country needing to get married for a green card. For every good story there are hundreds that are disasters. It all starts out looking like it is about love but it ends up being a con. She said that if they have no ability to get to the U.S. lawfully on their own, it is a red flag. I agree! Especially if you plan on living in the U.S., I advise that it is best to look closer to home for love where integrity, lifestyle, culture, family, friends, background, and personality traits can all be vetted before saying "I do." It takes serious work to vet for veracity of a romantic partner locally. It is near impossible for most people to have the resources to vet for veracity abroad.

A few of my attorney colleagues and I believe that this type of lengthy one-sided financial burden is so onerous that a policy change must be made. Perhaps, it can change to where the financial obligation ends at termination of marriage or it can be waived by the immigrating spouse or shared with the immigrating spouse. Other suggestions are that before signing to consent to that weighty obligation that an attorney should have to sign off along with the sponsoring U.S. Citizen spouse indicating he or she was fully advised of the legal ramifications. Another idea is to attach a separate fee to signing that sponsorship obligation to ensure the one signing it gives pause to the gravity of the agreement. So this one's for you my friends in the legislature! Or, those of you looking to champion a cause, this is a good one and will directly impact so many lives.

I also advise that the immigrating partner find their own lawful way to the U.S. so that the immigrating spouse controls their own status in their own hands, reducing the risk of being taken advantage of and the sponsoring U.S. citizen spouse doesn't bear the sole financial brunt of the sponsorship agreement. It is more balanced that way. It removes the air of doubt over your heads about the immigration motive for wanting to marry. So, if they can come lawfully as a student, a business person, or employee, the better. If you decide that sponsoring them is the best route to take, do yourself a favor and take time to be sure you want to be with them for the rest of your life. Have them live in your area for a period of time, so you know they know you and go live in their country as well to see if you appreciate them.

This is advice for men and for women. Sadly, I hear about men and women getting gamed for access to the United States. Some people have it down to a science and other family members are involved in the effort to scam you. This is an abusive practice and must stop.

Jani, 27 years old, was traveling to Morocco for school. She was in a unique master's program and was to be there for a semester. A sweet Moroccan girl connected her to her Moroccan family she could live with while there. The family were great hosts. They brought her into the family. They ate delicious meals together and made sure she had what she needed for her studies.

The family had a 22 year old son, Aamir, who also lived in the home, as customary in Moroccan families. He was helpful, funny, and fine. Jani did not fully understand it, but she could tell the family would hint that she and Aamir looked great together. Jani thought it was a moot point. She was there for school, he was younger than her, and she knew he was not a United States citizen, so he could not freely come to the U.S. She also did not see herself living in Morocco permanently.

After three months of being around Aamir and the family's consistent smiles and hints, Jani decided to give Aamir a chance. Aamir was already all in and asked Jani to marry him. He was a romantic and believed in love at first sight. Jani said she would have to wait to give her answer but she was a romantic too and thought he was sweet.

In the last few months of her time there she saw Aamir as a viable partner. When they discussed ideas about culture, Aamir was right on the same page. When they discussed aspects of having children, Aamir again agreed he wanted what Jani wanted. Jani was pleasantly surprised how much Aamir agreed with Jani's beliefs. Aamir also said he would love to live in Morocco, but knew that Jani preferred to live in the U.S. so out of love for her he would go with her there. That was comforting to Jani. She definitely knew that eagerness to get to the U.S. was a red flag, so she saw his reluctance as a good sign.

> *Aamir asked Jani to marry him again and Jani said yes. As they were preparing to do a small ceremony in Morocco before she left so she could start the visa process when she got home. Everything was going well. Then Jani noticed Aamir being rather secretive when he used his phone. She asked him about it and he said it was nothing and that she misunderstood. But something kept nagging at her. One day, Aamir left his phone on the table and Jani just took a look at it figuring she would not find anything. But, she found multiple text messages from other women. Some were in Morocco others were in other countries using pet names and talks of love and other raunchy messages.*
>
> *When Jani confronted Aamir and his family they said "what is the big deal?! Jani is a rich American and should help Aamir get out so he can send money back to the family." Jani was disgusted, heartbroken, yet grateful she found this out before going through with the wedding that Saturday. She went to stay in a hotel and made plans to head home.*

Or consider Nick and Svetlana:

> *Svetlana was from Russia. She and Nick met online and clicked! He traveled to Russia a couple of times to visit her. They were making plans to start a family when she moved to the U.S. Once her visa was approved she moved to Idaho. They got married and the first couple of years were great. Nick was making sure Svetlana acclimated to life in the U.S. He introduced her to all of his friends, showed her around, and taught her how to drive.*

> *As the months went on, Svetlana became a little quieter at times but said it was just because she missed her family. That made sense to Nick and he felt sad for her. He was looking forward to taking a trip back to Russia with Svetlana once her green card was shored up.*
>
> *But, after those first two years when the conditions were removed from her permanent residence card, Svetlana took off. Nick called her family back in Russia. One of the family members was kind enough to reveal to Nick that she went to live with her husband who was already in California. Nick could not believe it.*

Knowingly misrepresenting yourself is a crime – legally and morally.

> *Lisa met Paolo at the store she was working at while in college. He was tall, smart, and had a sexy accent. They got to talking and he said he graduated a few years before and worked in finance. Lisa was impressed. As she was studying business in the honors college, smarts were attractive and she liked to learn about different cultures. Paolo invited Lisa out one day and she accepted. They continued to get to know each other and eventually got married.*
>
> *Fifteen years after their marriage and two children later, a document from Immigration enforcement showed up at the house. It indicated that Paolo needed to immediately report.*
>
> *It turned out that Paolo was actually Gregorio. He had taken the identity of someone who had passed away, changed his name and had been living a lie under the radar for years. Paolo was given orders to return to his native country in South America.*

> *But, Lisa was a citizen and her children were too. It was a huge shocker for her, but she still loved her husband. So, instead of being separated, she and the kids decided to go with Gregorio to his country.*
>
> *A nightmare ensued from there. Gregorio became physically and emotionally abusive to her and the children. She had no idea who she married.*

Coming to America

If you are sure this is the person for you or if you are from another country and you are bringing your long established spouse over to be with you, seek legal advice to complete the visa process. There are a lot of forms in the immigration world and the fees are costly. This is something you want to do right the first time. Any mistakes may cause further delays, and when we are talking about immigration matters it could be additional months or years of delays. I know someone who went through the fiancé visa process, and it took about a year. I know another situation where the marriage visa process has taken five years. In the middle of that time the couple became pregnant and had a baby. They are still separated on different shores.

There are two main ways to marry someone who lives abroad.

- One would be to legally marry in the country where your future partner is a citizen and then, if you are sponsoring them, file for them as a spouse.
- The other way, has been made popular in the wild reality show 90 Day Fiancé. That is applying for a K-1 Fiance visa, bringing them to the U.S. and then within 90 days getting married or else their visa would expire and they would have to leave the country.

There are various reasons why a couple would choose one method over the other. It is a good idea to consult with an attorney to see what you qualify for and what would be best in your situation.

If you opt to go down the marriage route outside the U.S., keep in mind that just like it is important to understand the laws of your state it is doubly important to understand the marital laws of the other country. Some countries have laws that are similar to the U.S. while others are vastly different. There are some countries that require sons born in a marriage to remain with the father. There are other countries that do not give a woman the right to unilaterally petition for divorce. Whether you are a fan of those policies or not, to be legally savvy, you want to know what you are getting into. Furthermore, if the marriage contract and the entire court process could be in a language that you do not understand, I would recommend not getting married in that country unless you have a translator you trust. You do not want to inadvertently sign something you wish you hadn't.

Catch-22

Immigration can be a rough process for many people. There are cases where stateless Palestinians who were forced to flee their country wound up in Saudi Arabia. Because of the laws of Saudi Arabia, despite how long someone lives in the country they could not obtain full citizenship. It is based on Saudi lineage. So, there have been circumstances when they received a temporary residency that has to be regularly renewed. There was a case where a woman came to the U.S. and because of extenuating circumstances did not return to Saudi in time to renew her temporary residency. She stayed in the U.S. for over 20 years and lived an upstanding life starting a school and other community projects. Immigration enforcement caught up with her and she admitted the circumstance. But, now she did not have another home to return to because Palestine did not have an official citizenship, and she was a citizen of no other country. This is a sad situation and it would be a tricky situation to marry into and unadvisable if you foresee living in the U.S.

The coronavirus pandemic left some people stranded in the U.S. I received calls from people worried and wondering what they should do as their visitor visa was winding down but flights were banned back to their home country.

Sadly, there is turmoil in many countries where people do not feel safe to go out or have their children play in the street because of either organized crime violence, corruption, or war. Many flee with just a hope and a prayer to get to safety or get their children to safety and hope they will be granted asylum. Some people were brought to the U.S. as minors without documentation and the U.S. is the only home they know. Some people had the border cross them!

I am an advocate for compassionate immigration policies. I look forward to the U.S. being a model of excellence in this area. But, there is still a lot of work needed in this department. Also, I do not support any one manipulating or deceiving someone to take advantage of getting to America to reap the benefits that come with that. People deserve to have informed consent when getting married and to not be tricked or used. Don't get it twisted. Con artists, tricksters, and exploiters can be found in every group, nationality, race, religion, and gender. Be wise and legally savvy so you can protect yourself and have a peaceful life. What does love have to do with it if you are drowning in distress inside your own home?

This is information for you personally on what is out there so you can be legally savvy if you go down the road of marrying someone who is not already a U.S. citizen. I do not want you to be blindsided. Love is sweet but do not be a fool. Really manage your expectations on what your future would look like. As Dr. Aneesah emphasizes in her marriage preparation course, make sure you get and give informed consent about your status.

Whether you are the citizen or the immigrant, do not let just any person tell you about your rights. People will tell you all sorts of things. Consult with an attorney about your rights and responsibilities. Remember, your conversation is confidential and they are held to an ethical obligation to give you competent advice.

Criminal History

You want to know if your potential life-partner has a criminal record. This is not to condemn them or berate them. There are many reasons why someone may have a record. If they did their time, they have paid their debt to society. But you still do want to be aware though if there was any history or any pending charges. This is important because someone having a record can impact what apartment they can live in, what job opportunities may be available, and what school options may be open to them. For example, if your potential partner has a sex offender status you would be prevented from living near a school or in other family areas if you live together. Also keep in mind, your address would be listed as an address with a sex offender. That may affect your career or your community reputation.

There is a "ban the box" movement for jobs and colleges to not ask about an applicant's criminal history and there are felon friendly websites highlighting businesses that love giving second chances. But, the options as they are may not be what you expected. Some professions are still closed to those with a felony on their record. This despite the legal truism that once a sentence has been served, the debt to society is fully paid. A 2017 Huffington post article described these employment barriers as a resentencing of someone who served their full sentence. And certain professions like law or accounting may be closed if the crime included forgery or fraud. So, keep these things in mind and manage your expectations.

A thorough background check is a good idea. Use a professional one or check out police records and court documents on your own. These are public documents. This should only be done for serious prospects and not used to humiliate, blackmail, or injure the person in any way. It should just be for you to gather enough information to make a decision about the compatibility of this relationship for you.

A wise young woman who learned the importance of doing a background check in the hardest way said "better to dig up his past than have him dig up your grave." If he committed fraud in the past he'll commit it on you." This goes for men and women.

Unfortunately, we see this too often. There was a woman who met and married a man. She was successful in her career but was sweet and naïve about relationships. She did not know that even people who regularly attend religious services can have a dark side. Well, she married this person and he beat her profusely. The last I heard, he knocked out her teeth and her spirit.

One of the worst parts is that some people knew about his history for domestic violence but that information did not get to that woman in time.

Parental Status

You may be surprised by how much baby drama goes on. If your relationship leads to having a child, there are legalities to keep in mind. If your child is born out of wedlock and there is contention between you and the other party, beware. Men, if you have some reason to doubt your paternity, this will be a tough question to bring up. So be prepared that there will likely be a strain on your relationship or backlash. But, if you have reason to confirm, do it.

Kanye's lyric "18 years, 18 years, and on his 18th birthday he found out it wasn't his" bears out in everyday life. There was a tale of two dads. Dad one, Raheem, was with the baby's mother from the beginning. But he didn't know she was not exclusively with him. They were not married yet, but when they had the baby Raheem was overjoyed. He was at the birth and his name was on the birth certificate. He was a present dad and was actively raising his son. Five years later, dad two, Richie, showed up asserting the child was his. Raheem was devastated. Richie went through the court to order a paternity test, took it and it was confirmed Richie was the biological father. But, Raheem was not giving up that easily. He loved his son. His parents loved the baby and they were worried they would not be able to see their grandson again so they all lawyered up. Life can get legal really quickly.

Domestic Violence

As I write this, we are in the middle of a global pandemic. Sheltering in place with one's partner has tested even healthy relationships. Sadly, it has been a perilous experience for others. Domestic violence and toxic partners are raging. Not too far into the pandemic, I heard of a report of a woman who was murdered by her contemptible spouse. Her parents were devastated.

According to the National Domestic Violence Hotline:

> "An average of 24 people per minute are victims of rape, physical violence, or stalking by an intimate partner in the United States—more than 12 million women and men over the course of a single year."

The Hotline goes on to say, almost half of all women and men in the U.S. have experienced psychological aggression by an intimate partner in their lifetime (48.4% and 48.8%, respectively). In essence, the fight for justice is not just in the streets, but in the home.

Oftentimes I hear that someone did not get out of their abusive relationship because they did not know the legal steps or believed they could not afford to get out and safeguard their children or even beloved pets in the process. Again, oppression can occur outside as well as inside of the home.

Abuse or neglect of children also occurs. Protecting children is a principle in this country. If there are allegations of abuse or neglect, they are investigated by the local child welfare agency such as the Department of Child Safety (DCS). When a parent has had a child removed from their home, if an ongoing dependency case is still open, if they have another child during that time, it is very likely that child would also be removed from their care and put under the custody of the state.

Ben met Jen. He liked her. They both liked music and comic books. They started a sexual relationship almost immediately. Nine months later they had a child. Ben was still pretty excited and looking forward to parenting his child, despite the circumstances.

It was his first child, but it was Jen's third. Ben never saw Jen with her children. They were not in a cohabiting relationship. He assumed when she told him the kids were not with her for the weekend that they were probably with their dad or her parents.

Well, unfortunately, once the baby was born, child welfare was at the hospital to take the child into custody. Ben was confused.

The case worker explained that Jen had an open abuse or neglect case, known as a dependency, and the baby would go into the same foster home as her siblings. Ben is now looking for a lawyer to help him get custody of his child. He has a stable job at a hotel, but he is worried how much it is going to cost.

You may want to give it a couple of years before procreating to gauge who a potential partner truly is and, if they already have children, how those other children are managing.

Toxic and unfulfilling relationships have caused early health conditions, financial strain, more gray hairs, obesity, loss of faith, suicide, and homicide. This is no joke. Some people think certain treatment is not abuse if no one is getting hit. But it is certainly abuse and it is wrong. People do not talk about it and sometimes the silence perpetuates the crime.

I know a kind young woman recovering from years of an emotionally and psychologically abusive marriage with no other family history of breast cancer who will likely be getting a double mastectomy because her doctors found a lump. I have seen a talented woman devote herself to a marriage that literally almost killed her. Her husband unleashed a barrage of abuse upon her and topped it off with setting her house on fire while she showered. I have seen a desperate father uproot himself and move across the country everywhere the vindictive psychologically unstable mother had a whim to move, just to maintain connection with his child. I have seen beautiful loving people never experience true companionship because they are trapped in a loveless marriage with a spouse who started another family and has left them in limbo. I have seen the children of toxic marriages vow to never marry anyone or make reckless life decisions because they lost faith.

Emotional and psychological abuse remain difficult to present and prove beyond reasonable doubt in court. Physical scars weigh heavier and are more probative in court than the emotional ones even though they cut just as deep.

Community awareness campaigns have made a difference in educating the public. More than 225 specialty domestic violence courts exist in various jurisdictions around the U.S. and about the same globally. These courts seek to consolidate cases to bring broader protection for victims, hold perpetrators accountable, information sharing and link better to community resources.

Reach out to the National Domestic Violence Hotline at 1-800-799-7233 or thehotline.org for more information about red flags for abuse. Being legally savvy is a comprehensive approach to life.

Divorce

There is a large portion of life that is experienced behind closed doors. For some it could be satisfying and for others it could be highly wearisome. In the United States, half of first marriages end in divorce. With second marriages, 67% end in divorce. Additionally, nearly 74% of third marriages end in divorce.

Custody - Domestic and International

Sadly, some people will use your children as pawns and a tool to abuse you. This happens domestically all of the time. If you have an international component in your marriage also be aware. If you marry someone with citizenship in other countries, look into whether that country is a party to the treaty with The Hague Convention on Childhood Abductions. "This is a multilateral treaty, which seeks to protect children from the harmful effects of wrongful removal and retention across international boundaries by providing a procedure to bring about their prompt return and ensuring the protection of rights of access." You may also want to make some agreement or flag a child's passport that they may only leave the country with the written permission of both parents.

"This is my mother by a previous marriage."

If you have young children from the previous marriage you want to be extra mindful of this as you move forward with any relationship. An understanding ex-spouse can flip really quickly if he sees that the other spouse has moved on. You better believe that this new relationship will be meticulously raked over in court if there are still child custody hearings to be had. Your unofficial ex-spouse will want to know who

152 | ATTORNEY ZARINAH NADIR

the new person is, presume they are probably unfit, and may attempt to gain more parental control over the children.

In Summary

Unfortunately, not everyone you meet or fall in love with is trustworthy. If more preparation was given that would be one thing. Hopefully, this book will help to shift that tide. But, as of now, too many people are marrying people they did not take the time to know. We should not be marrying people we do not know, but sadly we do.

Hopefully, you will meet and be with someone whom you love and trust. But, do not be blind or leave it up to chance. Do not relinquish all of your agency. Marriage is best when it is a partnership. Each spouse individually contributing in a complementary way to uplift the pair. But, even in healthy relationships, it can take time to work out the kinks and get there.

These areas for conversation, discussed above, and a class or counselor can help you and your potential partner assess compatibility. An attorney will help you understand, under your personal circumstances, how marriage could legally impact you, your finances, your business, or children that you have or that are potentially yet to come.

Look at how much you have invested in college, your career, or a hobby in terms of the time, money, education, and professional services you put in to it and ask yourself, have you at least invested 2.5 percent of that, time, money, education and professional services to prepare yourself for a lifelong relationship. I am not talking about the wedding or accoutrements of the wedding. I am talking about in the relationship and in preparing yourself to be a great partner in a relationship and having a solid marriage. Reading this book counts toward that. So, congratulations and great job to you!

While not everything can be prevented, the legally savvy do not treat marriage like a crapshoot. They do not just roll the dice and hope they win. No! They do their part. They do not just hope. They work, and then have faith.

Legally Savvy Hacks

The Legally Savvy know...

- ✓ That everyone does not operate from the same value system
- ✓ That some people lie
- ✓ To do a background check before permanently coupling or getting married. Get receipts!
- ✓ To ask legally savvy questions before permanently coupling or getting married.
- ✓ If they reside in a community property state or a common law state
- ✓ It is better to stay out of trouble than to get out of trouble
- ✓ To always have some form of income as a protection from abuse.

By the pen and what they inscribe

— Quran Chapter 68,
Verse 1

CHAPTER 8

Skip the Fighting, Put it in Writing!

"The purpose of a writer is to keep civilization from destroying itself."
— Albert Camus

When we think about lawyers and the law, most of us think about criminal law. But contrary to popular understanding, the legal system is not solely about criminal justice. That is just one aspect of the overall legal system. It is probably more familiar to people because it receives the most media attention. When looking at media coverage, crime is sexy. We want to follow the salacious O.J. murder trial over Aretha Franklin's probate hearings. Or we become fascinated by a child kidnapping case over Halle Berry's child custody hearing.

The criminal justice system is also a lot more visual. We see the racing police car, we hear the siren, we see the flashing red lights, and we see the uniform on the scene. Other aspects of the law are more transactional. In a nutshell, that means these are dealings done on paper. But some of those deals could have consequences that make you wish you could call the police! For this reason, it is just as important to understand.

Part of me misses those days when we thought a pinky swear was an enforceable contract on the playground. We got a little older and we made deeper agreements like 'friends forever' and 'sisters before misters' while riding our bikes home from school. These are great things to say aloud to each other, but anything else should be written down. Research has shown that people have a tendency to forget things at various rates and the less relevant that thing is to them, the easier it is to forget. That is why the legally savvy write things down and do their part to ensure they follow the proper formality to keep things clear.

Estate Planning

One of the areas this can be most observed is around planning for your death. There are a number of legal tools you need to consider when planning.

According to the Caring.com 2021 Wills and Estate Planning survey, despite the COVID-19 pandemic, 2 out of 3 adults still do not have a will. COVID-19 has not changed the fact that almost two-thirds of Americans say that having a will is somewhat or particularly important, yet only one-third actually have estate planning documents. While many people say they were motivated by COVID-19 to see a greater need for a will and even take further steps, more than 1 out of 3 Americans still do not think it is important – or have not even thought about it at all.

Here is good news, however, the number of younger adults with a will or other estate plan has increased by 63% since 2020. This demographic was highly motivated by COVID-19 – so much so that those in the 18-34 age group are now more likely than those in the 35-54 age group to have an estate planning document. Overall, there are still only about a third of Black and Hispanics who have a will. However, that percentage has increased since 2020.

The survey went on to cite the following reasons for not having a will:

- They haven't gotten around to it,
- Don't have enough assets to leave anyone,

- They don't know how to get a will or a living trust, and
- It's too expensive to set up."

This comes down to an access and education issue. On a recent seminar, Lisa Hashem, co-host of the podcast *Muslim Women and Finance* reminded the audience that we cannot overlook that there have been systemic issues that have prevented certain groups from passing down generational wealth. This has led generations into getting out of the habit of preparing a will. Additionally, the more legally savvy people become the more they will understand that having a will is not just for the wealthy and there are resources to have attorneys prepare your will on a budget.

Your Will

This is known in legalese as your Last Will and Testament. It is important that you have a will that:

- Is in writing. Without a written document, those who are left behind may have honestly forgotten your instructions, forgotten part of them, or may have 'conveniently' forgotten.
- You do not know. People are funny around money! No matter how small it is. I have seen cases where the family was arguing over the scarves that still had mom's scent or the tacky pink flamingo that adorned Grandma's front lawn where everyone gathered for Sunday dinner. Something may not have monetary value, but when you pass, it ups in sentimental value.
- You sign and have witnessed to help ensure that your last wishes are known and implemented.
- Sets out who you want to be responsible to handle matters for your estate once you are dead (your Executor). You won't be around to remind anyone!

If there is a lot of money or potential money involved you may be setting your survivors up for a fight.

What Happens When Someone Dies Without a Will

On April 9, 2021, one of the most iconic Rappers and actors of my generation, DMX, passed away from a heart attack at the age of 50 in New York. DMX, whose real name is Earl Simmons, left behind 14 children, a fiancé, and no will. A battle has ensued as to who will take control of his estate which is valued at under $1 million dollars despite his chart-topping success. He was known to have challenges with substance abuse. But, it is not surprising to see stars make a comeback posthumously. So, his estate will likely see an increase over the years.

Two separate sets of his adult children each have attorneys and filed to be named as administrators of their father's estate. Desiree Lindstrom, DMX's fiancé since 2019 and the mother of his youngest child who is 5 years old, filed to be recognized as common law wife to DMX. The court denied her request based on the legal argument that she had no right under the law to make that request. If the judge had granted her request, however, she would have skipped to the front of the line as administrator for the estate.

Iconic hip hop producer and artist Swizz Beatz saw the commotion and during his eulogy for his friend mentioned it. He said, "the things that I'm witnessing from my brother's passing was a big educational thing for me to learn. I'm glad I got to see it at this age. A lot of people aren't your friends, a lot of people aren't your family." He went on to say "I need everybody to do a will. You have to do your will. You do not want strangers, blood suckers handling your business when you're not here." Well said.

Unclaimed Estates – You're My Daddy!

Despite having wealth and access to legal resources, DMX is not the only celebrity who passed without a will. Despite having massive wealth, some of them are just like the rest of us who procrastinate in sorting through their finances and other assets. The legendary Aretha Franklin, despite being urged by her long-time attorney, did not create a will or Trust to protect her multimillion dollar estate. Her four sons filed with the court to begin probate. However, her niece filed to be named administrator of the estate. That can get tricky.

Iconic Prince passed away at 57 years old in the elevator of his Paisley Park compound. He did not have a will. People came out of the woodwork claiming to be his secret wife, long lost child, or a distant relative. It was not until about a year after he died did a judge rule that his sister and five half-siblings were the heirs to his $200 million fortune.

In 2011, British soul singer Amy Winehouse was 27 years old when she died from alcohol poisoning, ending her brief yet impactful career. She did not have a will. The court determined that her parents were the rightful heirs of her multimillion-dollar estate. Her father was named as administrator of her estate. That sounds all fine and well until you realize her Oscar-winning documentary revealed she and her father had a reportedly hostile relationship.

If celebrities are facing these types of issues, how do you think the rest of us are managing?

Do not assume that if you do not designate something to be distributed someone will be altruistic enough to do it on their own. People get funny with money.

> *There was a woman, Tasha, whose father recently passed away. She was his only daughter. However, later in his life he married a woman, Jean. She was very professional, kind, and giving while Tasha's father was alive. When the father died, he did not leave a will with instructions for his current wife, Tasha's stepmother, on what he wanted to go to his daughter from his estate. And, Jean did not take it upon herself to share anything with Tasha.*

Timing of Your Will

When we turn 18 years old, we should have our own will. If we think about it, car accidents do not usually involve an older person on their deathbed. They are young people on the way to spring break or heading back from prom, or a middle-aged person driving home from work. So, getting a will done is not just a geriatric thing to do.

In the era of Covid-19, we saw the tide of health turn on a dime. We witnessed people who were well one day, get diagnosed the next day, and then sent to the hospital without any visitors permitted. There were issues trying to help people get their wills done when no one, not even notaries, could get to them.

We do not know the circumstances of our passing. It could be as a result of an accident, sickness, or natural causes. Popular comedian Tracy Morgan regularly jokes that he not only got into an accident, but it was by a Walmart truck, so it paid him out handsomely. Fortunately, he survived. But, what about a situation when the victim of the accident passed away. He could have not had any wealth in the estate, but once the incident was determined to be the fault of a negligent driver in a company vehicle, the estate now has financial assets that must be dealt with.

We cannot predict when or how we will die. Putting your final wishes in order in the proper way is something to not be delayed.

Updating Your Will to Keep It Current

An out-of-date will can be just as bad as no will at all. So the legally savvy take stock annually to make sure their will is still up to date. It is a good idea to update after every major life change which may include moving to a new state, buying a new home, starting a business, having another child, having grandchildren, getting married, or going through a divorce.

> *There was a business owner who was fortunate it was not too late to update their will. They needed to remove the current executor, the one responsible for distributing their property. The current executor was a former partner in their business who almost ensnared them into a horrific lawsuit because of some fraudulent business deals the executor was doing on the side.*

This plays out a lot with personal matters. One spouse makes a will while still married to their first spouse. They divorce, but never update the will. The last spouse has been cut out of the will and you and I both know the first spouse feels justified in claiming what bits there are to claim. The dead spouse is not there to face the fall out of not having expressed his wishes in writing. But as a legally savvy person, you want to do your part to keep your family on good terms and remembering you fondly – not cursing the day you were born!

Soundness of Mind

In order for a Will to be valid, it has to be done while you are "of sound mind and body." If it turns out your mental capacities are too diminished it can be too late to get a Will. With dementia and other mental health challenges that can zap your mental capacity, an attorney may have to decline to prepare your will.

In order to have a "sound mind" courts have held that the individual must fully understand the content and impact of their will. This means that they should understand what property they have and how it will be disposed of under the Will. The individual must also be able to understand who might have expectations of benefitting from the Will and what the nature of those claims might be against the estate.

Spouses and Wills

If you are married, each spouse would have their own separate will. Even if you are each leaving everything to the other, you still must have your own Will. I have heard from ladies, in particular, waiting on their husbands to get their Wills done. I do not usually hear husbands say they are waiting on their wives. Ladies, you do not have to prepare your Will at the same time as your spouse. It may be efficient, but if it is holding you up, go and get yours done. Remember, you may have some property that was given to you by your family that you want to keep in the family or you may have a charity to support that has personal significance to you.

Legal Guardianship of Minors

If you have children under 18 years of age, know that your Will is the only legal document in which you can name a guardian for them in the event that both parents die. If you do not name a guardian, a judge will appoint one for the children. This appointment will occur even though the judge does not know you or your child, or your sensible friend whom you would rather have raising your child than your impulsive sibling.

If you have children, I know that deciding who would raise your children as you would want is one of the hardest decisions to make. But, I implore you to make it. Someone you name will be better than a stranger. Imagine how devastating it would be for your child to endure losing you and moving to a stranger's home all at the same time.

On the other hand, you and your child may be so loved that conflict ensues as to who you would have wanted to care for the children. Imagine each set of grandparents vying to step in and fight for the children. At that point, child welfare and the courts would have to investigate who is fit. While that is getting sorted out the child may wind up in foster care.

> *One Thursday night, a delightful, community-engaged mother was dropping off two of her three wonderful teenage children to their jobs when an impaired car thief evading police sped through a red light at about 100 miles per hour and struck and killed this lovely family and wounded six others. Her 13 year old daughter, who was not in the car at the time, was the only surviving child. The mother did not have a Will. But she and the children were loved by many and there were at least four people planning to file for custody of the daughter.*

A lot of times I see that mothers may want to agree with their spouse on the guardian for the minor children. That is great if you can do it, but you do not have to. Whoever either of you pick is likely better than leaving it up to a stranger to decide. And, if it is any consolation, the way the law works in most states, the last one to die wins! Just keeping it light.

You've Got the Power

Having your powers of attorneys (POAs) in place is also important. While the will goes into effect at the time of death, powers of attorney are documents that help you live. Firstly, they give you the chance to designate someone you trust to make decisions for you while you are either unable or unavailable to make them for yourself. Secondly, they outline the scope of the agent's power and authority.

If you are in the hospital, in the military, studying abroad, going on pilgrimage, have a wild travel schedule, or would appreciate having family help with your affairs as you age, you will want to have a power of attorney in place.

There are two major types of powers of attorney:

- Health (mental and physical),

  You name a power of attorney and list what types of medical decisions they can make on your behalf if you are unable to speak for yourself.
  These areas may include consenting to mental health treatment, feeding tubes, blood transfusions, home health-care, and other lifesaving measures.

- Financial.

  This power of attorney helps you manage your financial decisions and is known as a durable power of attorney. It may include authorization to: pay your bills, gain access to accounts to pay your healthcare costs, hire an accountant or lawyer, apply for social security or veterans benefits to assist you if you are unavailable or incapacitated.

The legally savvy know the fact that they cannot do everything on their own. From time-to-time, as the Bill Withers' song says, *we all need somebody to lean on*. The legally savvy know that and prepare for it. They hope for the best, but figure at some point they may get sick or there may be an accident to the point where they are unconscious or incoherent. So, they do not want any delay in their care.

Who Should Be Your Power of Attorney

Your power of attorney does not have to be your spouse or a relative. You may have a friend who is cool under pressure, or skilled in medicine or finances, or who is closer to you than your family, whom you would prefer to make decisions on your behalf and who would be willing to serve in this capacity.

However, remember that unless you have this documented in a formal POA, a court will have to step in to designate someone if you are incapacitated and unable to make decisions on your own behalf. The legally savvy do their best to avoid that at all costs.

If you are married your spouse is usually your default. Note that a fiancé will not be a default and so if you want your fiancé to speak for you, this must be formally documented. If you are single your parents would be your default, regardless of whether or not you are a minor.

This is why it is so important, just like with a will, that powers of attorney and living wills should just be in place once you reach adulthood, 18 years of age. The legally savvy normalize these kinds of conversations in their homes. They see having these wishes in place do not just affect their death, but help them to live a more empowered life.

What Can a Person Designated as Your POA Do for You?

The person designated as your power of attorney can immediately step in, or with a doctor's approval if you prefer, and make sure that you get the care that you would ask for if you were able to ask yourself. The sooner those decisions can be made the better so that hopefully you can fully recover.

Your power of attorney for your finances could oversee that your financial affairs remain in order while you recover or are away. Prior to the prevalence of online banking there was a lot more that needed to be conducted face to face. But, still today, there are financial matters that if handled in person or telephonically, would require a verbal consent. If you have a dependable niece you want to help call the bank to find out your balances, help you dispute a fraudulent looking charge on your account, cancel your gym membership you no longer attend, or request a credit limit increase on your credit card you will need to have your power of attorney in place.

> *Femi was in her early 30's. She was generally healthy, but worked a high stress job. On the Sunday before she was to return to work after the weekend she had a massive heart attack and fell into a coma. She was in a coma for months. Fortunately, she recovered. However, when she came to the rest of her life was in a shambles. She was facing possible eviction for unpaid rent, she was behind on her car payment, and her cellphone had been disconnected. No one was designated to access her accounts and keep her bills up to date. Femi could have avoided these impacts if she had a financial power of attorney in place.*

A designated individual under a POA **only** has **those powers that you delegate to them** in the POA documents.

Updating Your Powers of Attorney

I often recommend to people who are going through a marriage dissolution to get their POA documents updated as soon as possible. I have heard of cases where a person passed away in the middle of an unfinished divorce and the soon to be ex was able to get back in and claim property rights as well as decision-making rights over the body.

The last person you would want to have control to speak for you is the person you are divorcing and until you are officially divorced, you are still married.

Powers of Attorney and Jail

The Covid-19 pandemic also exposed additional issues that families who have a justice system impacted relative face. When the stimulus checks were released, people who were incarcerated were also set to receive theirs. Some were looking forward to being able to help defray the expenses their family members had been absorbing to take their phone calls from jail and cover their commissary so they could have proper hygiene. When the checks arrived, without a power of attorney some families could not cash those checks and access the funds. And, because the power of attorney was not in place beforehand, it was nearly impossible trying to get the forms to them because they were incarcerated.

> *Denise worked with her adult son to get his power of attorney in place. She did not know she would need it so soon. A week after the POAs were all in place, Denise found out that her son had been arrested on a warrant while he was out. A couple of months later, Denise received notice that her son's items, that he had with him while he was being arrested, were at the police station's holding location for a limited time. She was told she could pick up the items as long as she had a POA to do so. She had one in place! Imagine if she did not. When the stimulus checks were sent, Denise used the same POA to get her son's $1,200 check cashed! That money came in handy to deal with some of the daily expenses of life with an incarcerated family member.*

Temporary Powers of Attorney for College or University

As soon as your child turns 18 years of age, they are an adult. Because of privacy laws, parents, absent powers of attorney in place, will not be able to speak to their children's doctors or school administrators without their consent. So, before they head off to college, help them get their affairs in order.

The legally savvy do their part to assist their family in having their documents in place. Make it their "adulting" graduation gift! They may not thank you until later – heck, throw in a couple of cash gift cards to sweeten the pot -but this will be a relief for you and them.

We have all heard stories of students going off to college and having interactions with the law from as innocuous as a traffic ticket to as traumatic as sexual assault altercations or alcohol related debacles. While they are an adult, they may still appreciate having the assistance of mom and dad. Having these documents in place can create some ease in an already difficult situation.

> *There was a college student, Ali, who became ill in the middle of his freshman year in college. It looked like he was going to be behind on his classes. His parents went down to the registrar office to try to negotiate Ali's withdrawal from the courses before it would count as a fail, ruining his pre-med GPA.*
>
> *The registrar had to notify the parents that they were not able to give them any information about Ali's grades without his consent since he was over 18 years old.*

Final Thoughts on Powers of Attorney

On a sad note also, the person who has this power to pull the plug may also be the one who put you in the hospital. So, be aware of these forms and designate someone who has your best interest at heart.

Living Wills

You also want to have a living will in place. A living will is a document that provides the extent of life saving measures you want taken on your behalf. In more simple terms it sets out the limitations on medical treatment and under what circumstances medical treatment is to end.

You may remember Terri Schiavo. Sadly, most of us know her name because she did not have a living will in place. She was newly married and just in her twenties when, in 1990, she suffered from severe cardiac arrest. She fell into a coma and was in a persistent vegetative state. She was kept alive with a feeding tube. Her husband said that his wife would not have wanted to live that way and asked the doctors to pull the plug and let her go in peace. Her parents believed he did not have her best interest at heart and fought to keep her alive. From 1998 to 2005, the family duked out the issue in court. After years of costly court procedures and medical expenses, it went all the way to the Supreme Court, and they finally ruled in favor of the husband's position. This case serves as a wakeup call that a simple document can prevent family chaos.

Get Down to Business

As entrepreneurs, various agreements are made throughout the course of business. Prior to starting a business you may want to get feedback on an idea. Remember, sharing it with your attorney will inherently be confident. But, if you have friends or potential beta users you would like to test it out, then prior to sharing the idea you may want to have a non-disclosure agreement or NDA signed.

Have you ever been in a situation where a friend shares some information with you but did not explicitly say it was a secret? So, you are not sure. Well, an NDA takes the guesswork out of it. An NDA advises the other person that the details about the project are confidential, should remain confidential, and he potential penalties for its disclosure.

When making any agreements about compensation, even if it is to do a small job at your office or on a project, write it down. Consult with an attorney as to how detailed the document should be. An email spelling out the arrangement may be sufficient but double check. The bottom line is, whether it is a personal or a business matter, whether it is between friends or strangers, the legally savvy write it down.

Legally Savvy Hacks

The Legally Savvy know…

- ✓ To skip the fighting, put it in writing
- ✓ To have updated estate planning documents including a will, powers of attorney, and a living will
- ✓ That whether it is between friends or strangers, write agreements down.
- ✓ Being Legally Savvy is not a given, it is a choice. You have to decide to be legally savvy.

Give us the tools, and we will
finish the job.

— Winston Churchill

CHAPTER 9

Lawyer Up

A good tool improves the way you work. A great tool improves the way you think.

— Jeff Duntemann

We live in a post-industrial society and are faced with myriad complexities. Gone are the days when we could secure major business arrangements with a handshake. And although we all know someone who freely gives advice like their opinions are a dime a dozen or who acts like they know everything, the legally savvy only get legal advice from attorneys. Attorneys are an essential tool to utilize to improve your quality of life and improve the way you think.

There are a number of reasons why it matters that you get legal advice only from attorneys. Given the complexity of our world, we cannot all be experts at everything.

In our society, when we have health issues we turn for help to the professionals who study healthcare, such as doctors and nurses. When there are mental health challenges, the professionals who assist with this are psychologists, psychiatrists, counselors, and social workers. To solve infrastructure issues, we turn to engineers.

To protect the public and ensure that the individuals we entrust with these responsibilities operate to a common standard of competence and keep their professional practice above board, we have the laws and regulations that govern these professions in our society and often require licensing and ongoing professional education. These laws and regulations set out our rights and our responsibilities on an individual and communal level in regards to that profession.

As a result, it has become more exclusive to enter these professions in terms of educational and licensing requirements. On the other hand, those requirements have been a protection for our society. When you have a license to lose, that is an extra check on one's moral fortitude. You do not hand out advice like it is candy! You may research before giving advice. You will want to know more details about the client's situation so you can fully understand the complexities. You feel the weight of the repercussions of losing your profession if you act unethically or engage in malpractice.

There are a few professions that study the law. But the profession that studies laws and how to counsel you on how they apply to you are lawyers. We have discussed previously in the Guide that attorneys have a broad scope of expertise that can be of assistance to us and that lawyers are not just for bad things. You can refer back to that section to refresh on the broad scope of what attorneys do.

Why and When to Work with an Attorney

- *Professional Regulation:* In the case of legal matters, with only a few exceptions, only licensed attorneys are authorized to give legal advice. When others try to do it, they may be cited for the unauthorized practice of the law.
- *Legal Advice Standards:* In the same way that you would not want a plumber to operate on your brain, or want a dentist to wire the electricity in your new home, the ramifications of obtaining legal advice from someone who is not trained or

licensed to practice law can be very serious. To an untrained eye a serious issue might appear to be trivial and there is little incentive for an individual without a license to lose to ensure that the advice they might give you is actually the way the law works.

In law, like other professions, expertise matters. While studying and practicing in a field a professional gains a unique vantage point that helps you. You don't know what you don't know. To give you some perspective, while I was in law school studying statutory interpretation, I can remember that we spent two weeks just studying the word, *shall* and how it can be interpreted!

- *Ethical Oversight and Insurance:* Have you ever gotten bad advice? And the person who gave it to you was nowhere to be found when you had to face the music. Because attorneys are all required to pass licensing examinations, maintain malpractice insurance and have trust requirements and codes of ethics that they must meet, this provides clients with a safety net against sub-standard legal advice being provided by a licensed lawyer. The oversight function provided by the Bar Associations for that jurisdiction also ensures that clients have a governing body to register complaints with and consequences might include the loss of a license for an individual found to have breached their professional requirements.

To understand whether or not your issue could benefit from legal counsel requires an analysis done by an attorney, someone who has studied the area, has seen how these issues play out and knows the laws behind it. In order to obtain an accurate assessment, let an attorney tell you if you need an attorney.

The best person to ask if you need a lawyer is a lawyer! Do yourself a favor and run legal questions by lawyers. It will save you time, stress, and money in the long run! The attorney can tell you if that cough looks like "legal pneumonia" or if you will require "legal surgery" like going to court.

The Right to an Attorney and Its Limitations

When we study Miranda rights and get to that part about having an attorney assigned to us, we must know that is highly limited. It is important to know that constitutionally an attorney is only assigned to you if you are facing loss of your freedom, as in a criminal case, or loss of your child as in a juvenile law case. There is no other constitutional right that promises you a right to an attorney.

That means you do not have a right to have an attorney assigned to you for your nasty divorce or if you are being evicted from your apartment. You do not have the right to an attorney assigned to you if you were fired or if you felt you were shorted on your paycheck. Nor, do you have the right to have an attorney assigned to you when you are experiencing domestic violence or decide to start a non-profit. That means for the vast majority of our lives we are on our own to find and secure our own legal counsel.

Costs Associated with Retaining an Attorney

The practice of law is expensive. That is why attorneys are expensive. Depending on their type of practice or region of the country, some attorneys are more expensive than others. Attorneys typically charge by the hour and $300 to $400 per hour is common. Some of my colleagues on the east coast charge twice that. Yet, the legally savvy know they and their families deserve to have the assistance and expertise of attorneys.

Unfortunately, the traditional practice of the law has price locked out the rest of us from having this critical access. Justice Earl Johnson, Jr. agreed. He said:

"Except for the few that legal services lawyers can represent, poor people have access to American courts in the same sense that the Christians had access to the lions when they were dragged, unarmed, into a Roman arena."

Ouch! That is social injustice. Part of social justice is equity in access. If someone is not able to have a fair shot at something simply because they do not have the funds to access it, then injustice occurs.

I went to law school to help remove barriers to accessing justice. But my fees became a barrier to the very people I went to law school to help. Even those who had the means to swipe a check at that moment would not typically have the funds it would take to put a retainer down to use me as often as they should be using me. Having a completely pro bono practice is just simply not sustainable either.

Again, it is found that Americans are foregoing the legal help they need because of cost, access and trust issues. So, it is not that the rest of us do not need to use attorneys, it is that most of us do not know a better way to get access. But, when we know a better way we still need to know how to be legally savvy. We need to be able to recognize quicker when to not just chock an issue up to "bad luck" but rather when an issue may have a legal component. When we do we will really use attorneys like the super wealthy do and as such reap the benefits the super wealthy reap - the 4 C's and an E - that is being:

- Confident,
- Competent,
- Capable,
- Calm, and
- Empowered

Collectively, we must work on increasing our legal savviness. You deserve that. Your family deserves that. Your community deserves that.

Retainers, Legal Plans, Legal Aid and Pro Bono

The legally savvy maintain ready access to attorneys who practice in most areas of the law and in all jurisdictions of their country. They know that most issues are complex and can span multiple areas of law and even cross state lines. If you live in Los Angeles today, but grew up in Chicago, went to college in Boston, and have lots of family in Atlanta you need multi-state legal access. You may have landlord/tenant questions for your apartment in LA, received a traffic ticket while going to visit old friends in Chi-town, have a company from B-Town saying you still owe them money, and have family property in Hotlanta you have been helping your mom get for the last 20 years when gramps passed without a will.

You want to incorporate regular consulting with an attorney in your life and having them watch over your back during life stages. It is like having an insider tip!

The legally savvy do not have to get ready; they stay ready.

With on-going access to attorneys, you will notice your stress reduce because you can get answers to questions that have been weighing you down. Even if it is not the answer you want to hear, at least you can face it and move on rather than carry that pit of doubt in your stomach. That is empowering.

The only way I have seen this work out is in one of two ways.:

1. The super wealthy have put multimillion dollar retainers down at large multi-state law firms. According to Georgetown Law, these are law firms that have multiple locations or consist of 100 attorneys or more.

2. Legal Plan Programs: While the super wealthy can independently secure that level of access, for the last 50 years the rest of us have done so collectively through legal plan programs. Prior to 1972 in the U.S. this was almost unheard of.

So, if the multi-million dollar retainer at a large law firm is out of the budget for you now, you will want to join a legal plan program.

There are legal plan programs in place that have already negotiated with large and mid-size law firms that give you access to quality firms throughout the country. Members of these programs only pay a small monthly fee for robust pre-negotiated benefits and receive an exclusive member only discount on additional legal services.

In the United States and Canada, the best program I have seen is LegalShield. They have been around for about fifty years and have the best delivery model and service standards in the industry. Additionally, they are the only organization in the United States that provides 24/7 access to attorneys nationwide for emergencies that are legal in nature.

That is the legal plan program that I have used for the last decade. Yes, even attorneys use attorneys too. Doctors have health coverage, right!

There are other legal plan programs. Some jobs offer these types of programs as an employee benefit. I recommend getting a legal plan program from an independent agent when possible. That would provide you with the most flexibility in usage.

Back in 2008, **The National Association of Attorneys General (NAAG)**, the nonpartisan national forum where the 56 attorneys general of the United States collaborate joined the American Bar Association affirming their support of legal plan programs. In one of their coveted resolutions where they collectively unite to throw their support for an area of justice they emphasize they support legal plan programs because they:

1. Are important to maintaining the confidence in our justice system and the rule of law.
2. Efficiently and inexpensively provide preventative legal services to low and middle income Americans.
3. Ease the burden on overtaxed government programs.

4. Enhance productivity by allowing employees to focus on their jobs, not their legal troubles.

I thoroughly agree with them as this is what I have observed as an attorney, a community organizer, and in my personal life.

Alternatives to Legal Plans

If you are not at the level yet where you can maintain a monthly legal plan program then you have to hustle a bit.

- Search for a legal aid agency in your area.
- Check with the local law school to see if there is a pro bono clinic, or
- call your state's bar association to see if they have a modest means program.

If the program is not totally pro bono or free, then it will likely be more than just having a legal plan program. But get in where you fit in until you are able to upgrade yourself.

In these programs you are still working with good lawyers you just really have to plan far ahead as they typically have very limited resources and have to triage for the most severe cases first. Do not be surprised if it takes several days to a week to get a call back.

But do what you have to do. I respect that. Then, work on getting to a monthly legal plan program as soon as possible. That will save you time, stress, and money in the long run.

Legal Plans in Other Jurisdictions

If you move to another country, scope out the scene to see if there is a legal plan program available as a convenient way to get access to attorneys. European countries like Germany have had legal plan programs available to join way before the U.S.

Let me tell you, in hindsight, I would have liked to have had a program to join while I was a student studying abroad in Mexico. We signed up for health insurance and I made sure I had a gym membership. But legal access was not even offered! Thankfully, everything went smoothly for me while I was there.

But it is not out of the question to imagine a situation where I could have used advice from an attorney. I remember that one of my classmates was arrested one night while hanging out and we were scrambling to find out who could help him. That was not a legally savvy approach.

If you are going to spend any significant time in another area, the legally savvy thing to do is to have previously identified legal counsel to assist. You would not want to waste precious time trying to find someone. Remember, stay ready.

Conclusion

We have our rights. But, make no mistake, being legally savvy is a choice. You can have resources but not know how to use them. You could have a Ferrari, but if you do not know how to drive it, what's the point? So, regardless of your level of legal savviness, there is always more we can learn. I continue to learn too. So, congratulations on using this book as a tool for legal empowerment.

It has been said, if you do not know your rights you do not have any. That is because in this world, the reality is for the most part, people are not worried about making sure you have your rights. They are too consumed with worrying about themselves and their family. It is up to us to know how far we can go and our limits. It is okay. Put your own oxygen mask on first.

There are individuals and businesses who bank on your ignorance. It feels wrong but a lot of times it is legal. Now, you have the tools to help yourself, your family, and your legacy. Remember, being cocky is not what being legally savvy means. It means you can more vibrantly and professionally engage in love, life, and business.

Incorporate regular consulting with an attorney and experience the peace of mind that comes with them having your back throughout your various stages of life. It is a marvellous feeling utilizing your time, a precious finite commodity, on things other than stress, waiting on hold, tracking down supervisors or arguing. You will notice a reduction in anxiety because you can get answers to questions that have been weighing you down. Experience the 4C's and an E - be confident, competent, capable, calm and empowered.

Let's play team! It is important to know our rights and how to exercise them. When the rest of us are legally savvy that helpfully alleviates pressure on all of the advocates and advocacy groups out there. The more of us who can proactively handle our affairs and prevent legal catastrophes, the more those limited resources are freed up to help the super indigent or most serious cases.

Then as individuals, families, and communities it is important that we support the movement of having a legally savvy community. Enough slick and crooked people have information and use it to exploit. The savvier the rest of us become, the more we can remove the target from our backs and off the backs of our community members.

Will everyone become legally savvy? I hope so! I think it is high time for a change. I can see it now - the day when contracts are drafted with clarity and consideration and they are passed to the rest of us accompanied with a gentleman's courtesy and the words "go ahead, take a few days to sign it. I know you'll want to have your attorney review that with you." And we send it over to our attorney, and she goes over our rights and responsibilities about it and says it looks great. If she points out one area to clarify we simply go ask the drafting party to clarify it. They do so with humility and grace and we have ourselves a wonderful deal.

I envision a day when African Americans, Black, and Brown people can drive at peace in any neighborhood at any time of the day. Not necessarily because attitudes about racism have all vanished, but because overreaching law enforcement and lay abusers of the system are on notice that this community knows their rights, they have lawyers, and they know how to use them.

I can see more peaceful marriages, artists feeling valued because contracts protect their rights, parents are better able to navigate the school and medical systems to see their children do not fall through the cracks, and the courts are not as utilized because terms are better understood and more fairly put in place.

This is what the hacks and principles in this book are designed to do. It is to elevate our entire communities, one person at a time. Being legally savvy helps to break you free from the shackles of oppression. It is like what that old Saturday morning public service announcement used to say, "the more you know, the more you grow."

Take Action

1. If you do not have a legal access plan, get one. If you already have one, use it.
2. Write down one thing you could call an attorney about right now. Remember, legal issues do not get better with time. Lawyers are not just for bad things. Now call your law firm!
1. Take one lesson you learned each time you read this book and pass it on to a loved one. Do not keep this information a secret.

Let's see our communities thrive and be legally savvy!

Legally Savvy Hacks

The Legally Savvy know to:

✓ Only take legal advice from lawyers.
✓ Join a legal plan program or hire a multi-state law firm with 24/7 emergency access.
✓ Practice being legally savvy.

What's Next?

ow that you're legally savvy and have begun to take control of your love, life and business, what's next?

Get lawyered up!

Protect yourself and get legal access. If you are in the United States and Canada, contact me for my favorite resources and affiliate links at zarinah@belegallysavvy.com.

Get Featured!

I would love to hear your wins practicing the *Legally Savvy* hacks and highlight your story on a future blog or podcast. Sharing the stories helps us all. If you are interested in having your story featured, please contact me or post on social media using the hashtags #legallysavvy and #belegallysavvy.

GET IN TOUCH

For more information, private appointments, to book a speaking engagement, or to get lawyered up please reach out through the following methods. Zarinah would love to connect!

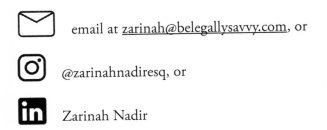

✉ email at <u>zarinah@belegallysavvy.com</u>, or

⬡ @zarinahnadiresq, or

in Zarinah Nadir

References

"10 Interesting Facts about Marriage." IMOM, 30 Apr. 2021, www.imom.com/10-interesting-facts-about-marriage/.

"10 Most Expensive Law Schools | the Short LIST: Grad School | US News." U.S. News & World Report, U.S. News & World Report, www.usnews.com/education/best-graduate-schools/the-short-list-grad-school/articles/most-expensive-law-schools.

"2021 Wills and Estate Planning Study." Caring.com, www.caring.com/caregivers/estate-planning/wills-survey/.

"Arizona Bar EXAM INFORMATION: Important Dates & Guidelines." Bar Exam Info, 10 July 2020, bar-exam.info/state-bar-info/arizona-bar-exam/#:~:text=How%20much%20does%20the%20Arizona,receive%20the%20required%20character%20report.

"Attorney David McCarville Speaks about the Importance of Designating a Power of Attorney." Arizona PBS, 27 May 2021, azpbs.org/horizon/2021/05/mental-health-and-the-importance-of-power-of-attorney/.

"Ban the BOX: Opening the Door to College for FELONS | Best Colleges | US News." U.S. News & World Report, U.S. News & World Report,

www.usnews.com/education/best-colleges/articles/
ban-the-box-opening-the-door-to-college-for-felons.
"Bill and Melinda Gates Are Divorcing with No PRENUP – Why
Having an Exit Plan Is Critical." LegalShield USA, www.
legalshield.com/blog/divorce/bill-and-melinda-gates-are-
divorcing-no-prenup-why-having-exit-plan-critical.
Conducted by Decision Analyst, Inc. Commissioned by LegalShield,
2012, *The Legal Needs of American Families A Research Study.*
"Disbarred Lawyer Sentenced to 5 Years in Prison for Wire Fraud and
Aggravated Identity Theft." *The United States Department of Justice,*
1 Nov. 2019, www.justice.gov/usao-wdwa/pr/disbarred-lawyer-
sentenced-5-years-prison-wire-fraud-and-aggravated-identity-theft.
"Domestic Violence Statistics." The Hotline, 15 June 2021, www.
thehotline.org/stakeholders/domestic-violence-statistics/.
"Former JP Morgan Chase Bank Employee Sentenced to Four
Years in Prison for Selling Customer Account Information."
The United States Department of Justice, 10 Aug. 2018, www.
justice.gov/usao-edny/pr/former-jp-morgan-chase-bank-
employee-sentenced-four-years-prison-selling-customer.
"Global Insights on Access to Justice 2019." World Justice Project,
world
justiceproject.org/our-work/research-and-data/global-insights-
access-justice-2019.
"Kent Man Who Stole Identity to Work While Collecting Disability
Sentenced to Prison." *The United States Department of Justice,* 1
Apr. 2016, www.justice.gov/usao-wdwa/pr/kent-man-who-stole-
identity-work-while-collecting-disability-sentenced-prison.
"Law Firms." Law Firms, www.law.georgetown.edu/your-life-career/
career-exploration-professional-development/
for-ll-m-students/starting-your-job-search/
explore-your-career-options/practice-settings/law-firms/.
"Pandemic Disrupts Justice System, Courts." American Bar
Association, www.americanbar.org/news/abanews/aba-news-ar-

chives/
2020/03/coronavirus-affecting-justice-system/.
"Prenuptial." *Hello Prenup*, www.helloprenup.com/prenup-clauses/.
"Resolution in Support of the Concept of Prepaid Legal
Services Plans", National Association of Attorneys
General, Providence, Rhode Island June 17-19, 2008
"State Courts." America's Courts and the Criminal Justice System, by
David William Neubauer and Henry F. Fradella, Cengage, 2019.
"Tacoma Woman Sentenced to 27 Months in Prison for 7-Year Public
Assistance Fraud Scheme." *The United States Department of Justice*,
18 Nov. 2020, www.justice.gov/usao-wdwa/pr/tacoma-woman-sen-
tenced-27-months-prison-7-year-public-assistance-fraud-scheme.
"The Ruling Is in: The Eviction Moratorium Is out. What Does
This Mean for Renters & Landlords?" LegalShield
USA, www.legalshield.com/blog/landlordtenant/ruling-evic-
tion-moratorium-out-what-does-mean-renters-landlords.
"U.S. Muslim Leaders Say FBI Pressuring People to
Become Informants." Los Angeles Times, Los Angeles
Times, 3 Nov. 2014, www.latimes.com/nation/
la-na-muslims-fbi-20141103-story.html.
"Worcester Man Indicted for Using Stolen Identities to Open Bank
Account and Attempting to Purchase $83,000 Sports Car."
The United States Department of Justice, 21 June 2021, www.
justice.gov/usao-ma/pr/worcester-man-indicted-using-sto-
len-identities-open-bank-ac count-and-attempting-purchase.
Aquino, Alyssa. "Harvard's Rejection Of Chelsea Manning AND
Michelle Jones Proves Academia's Intolerance." HuffPost,
HuffPost, 15 Sept. 2017, www.huffpost.com/entry/harvard-col-
lege-doesnt-honor-felons_b_59bc2d5ee4b06b71800c392a.
Blas, Lorena, and Andrea Mandell. "7 Legendary Stars Who Died
without Wills: ARETHA Franklin, Prince and More." USA
Today, Gannett Satellite Information Network, 22 Aug. 2018,

www.usatoday.com/story/life/people/2018/08/22/legendary-stars-who-died-without-wills-aretha-franklin/83550424/.

Brown, Preezy. "DMX's Family MEMBERS Battle for Control of His Estate." VIBE.com, 21 June 2021, www.vibe.com/music/music-news/dmx-family-estate-control-battle-1234621580/#!

Bureau, US Census. "National Population Totals: 2010-2019." The United States Census Bureau, 20 Apr. 2021, www.census.gov/data/tables/time-series/demo/popest/2010s-national-total.html.

e-Vision.nl, The Netherlands. "Child Abduction Section." HCCH, www.hcch.net/en/instruments/conventions/specialised-sections/child-abduction.

Frazier v. Cupp, 394 U.S. 731 (1969)

French, Laurence Armand. "Policing American Indians: A Unique Chapter in American Jurisprudence." Routledge & CRC Press, Taylor & Francis Group, www.routledge.com/Policing-American-Indians-A-Unique-Chapter-in-American-Jurisprudence/French/p/book/9780367871727.

Graham, Graham. "Some U.S. Police Train for Just a Few Weeks, in Some Countries They Train for Years." CBS News, CBS Interactive, 11 June 2020, www.cbsnews.com/news/police-training-weeks-united-states/.

Holmes, Dave. "The Rise of Elevated Stupidity." Esquire, 2021, pp. 17–19.

Jessica Arnold, Louisa Ballhaus, et al. "20 Most IMPORTANT Celebrity Lawsuits over the Years." SheKnows, 8 Jan. 2021, www.sheknows.com/entertainment/slideshow/8731/biggest-celebrity-lawsuits/20/.

Kassin, Saul. "It's Time for Police to Stop Lying to Suspects." The New York Times, The New York Times, 29 Jan. 2021, www.nytimes.com/2021/01/29/opin-ion/false-confessions-police-interrogation.html.

Limbong, Andrew. "Rapper and ACTOR Dmx Dead at 50." NPR, NPR, 9 Apr. 2021, www.npr.org/2021/04/09/984274079/rapper-and-actor-dmx-dead-at-50.

Published by Statista Research Department, and Aug 6. "U.S.: Number of Lawyers 2007-2021." Statista, 6 Aug. 2021, www.statista.com/statistics/740222/number-of-lawyers-us/#:~:text=How%20many%20lawyers%20are%20in,2015%20figure%20of%201.3%20million.

Rhode, Deborah L. "Law Is the Least Diverse Profession in the Nation. and Lawyers Aren't Doing Enough to Change That." The Washington Post, WP Company, 1 Mar. 2019, www.washingtonpost.com/posteverything/wp/2015/05/27/law-is-the-least-diverse-profession-in-the-nation-and-lawyers-arent-doing-enough-to-change-that/.

Rose, Jordan. "Watch Swizz BEATZ Deliver Heartfelt Speech At Dmx's Memorial Service." Complex, Complex, 25 Apr. 2021, www.complex.com/music/swizz-beatz-dmx-speech-memorial-service.

S., Durvasula Ph.D Ramani. *Don't You Know Who I Am?*. Post Hill Press, 2019.

Shelton, Jacob. "The Most Interesting Things You Could Buy for $100k.", 24 June 2016, www.ranker.com/list/things-you-can-buy-for-100k/jacob-shelton.

Smith, Emily. "Battle Kicks off over RAPPER DMX's Estate." Page Six, Page Six, 19 June 2021, pagesix.com/2021/06/19/battle-kicks-off-over-rapper-dmxs-estate/.

Thalheimer, W. (2010, April). How Much Do People Forget? Retrieved June 21, 2021, from http://www.work-learning.com/catalog.html

The Noble Quran. Trans. By Dr. Muhammad Taqi-ud-Din Al-Hilali and Dr. Muhammad Muhsin Khan, Chapter 3, Verse 120. Darussalam, 1997.

Victor v. Victor, 866 P.2d 899, 177 Ariz. 231 (Ariz. App. 1993)

Walls, Barbranda Lumpkins. "Survey: 60% of Americans Lack Will or Estate Planning." AARP, 24 Feb. 2017, www.aarp.org/money/investing/info-2017/half-of-adults-do-not-have-wills.html.

Weiss, Debra Cassens. "Lawyer Count in US Increases 14.5% from Decade Ago; These 5 States Have Highest Number of ACTIVE ATTORNEYS." ABA Journal, www.abajournal.com/news/article/lawyer-count-in-the-us-increases-14.5-from-a-decade-ago.

Wisely, John. "Aretha Franklin Didn't Leave a Will; Here's What Will Happen to Her Estate." USA Today, Gannett Satellite Information Network, 22 Aug. 2018, www.usatoday.com/story/life/music/2018/08/22/aretha-franklin-estate-fortune/1063513002/.

Acknowledgements

I am grateful the Creator has carried me through my first literary journey. This has been an exceptionally trying time for me as it has been for so many others. But, God curated the perfect condition for me to write this book. As God promised "verily in difficulty, there is ease." I have understood the meaning of this Quranic injunction during this year more than ever before.

To all those men and women, who have suffered the indignities of injustice to ensure future generations did not have to or to just survive, you are freedom fighters and I see you.

To all of the lawyers and advocates who are working to bring more equal access to justice to the rest of us in large and small ways, I thank you for your courage and persistence. Consider me your partner.

I thank my parents who supported me, literally and figuratively, through law school and every subsequent step of my career. They are two of my best friends and willingly listened to aspects of the law I found fascinating and encouraged me to teach others. I am delighted to be my mother's co-conspirator in community building. She was my first mentor and is my closest advisor. My father fuels me with his positivity and has always encouraged me to pursue my big unconventional success path. My parents are true blessings and instrumental in me completing this book from the dinners they had ready for me to reading every iteration of this manuscript. I thank all of my family for their love, reminders that our family's legacy brims with black excellence and that social justice is woven into the DNA of our culture and faith.

Thank you to my beta readers and friends, the perceptive and sharp Tasneem Halloum, Amirah Ismail and Jacki Shoyeb, and to my brilliant brother and diversity and inclusion consultant, Dahir Nasser who patiently edited sections for me amid his international *hijra*.

Thank you to my social justice intern Megan Looney, Nancy Speidel and iSAW. While pursuing her master's in social justice, Megan provided me with some pivotal research for this manuscript. You are going to make a fantastic lawyer one day. I am grateful to have collaborated with the accomplished Nancy and iSAW. Nancy helped me to think locally as well as globally.

Thank you to my mentors Tanisha Morgan, Harold Branch, Craig Hepner, Tara Paustenbach, and Kai Deering for giving me some of my earliest platforms to teach people how to be legally savvy.

Thank you to the indefatigable Holly Marshall who believed in me as a young college student and gave me my first law-related job in her law firm. There, I was able to witness the true meaning of what a lawyer fighting for justice looks like.

Friendship is one of the riches of life. Thank you to all of my beloved friends who have prayed for me or lifted me up with words of encouragement to complete this book. Specifically for this project, thank you Cathy Perez and Ken Evans for your relentless encouragement. Thank you Sister Karen Hadley, Marci Hadely-Mairel, Nicole Hadley, Amal Fayad, and Aaron Blau for letting me bounce ideas off of you to finesse certain key sections of my book. Thank you to my branding stylists Sumaya Abdul-Quadir, Nure Elatari, and Alesia Wilson. Your art is generosity and aesthetics.

I thank my team, clients, and members who trust me with the significant moments in your life. It is an honor to work with you.

This book would not have been completed without my publisher, coach, and fellow "golden one" Zarinah El-Amin who provided gentle yet unwavering assistance with the tools and timelines to birth this project. Thank you for connecting me to my editor, the meticulous, amazingly focused, and former attorney, Fiona Mackintosh and the entire design team. Thank you to my fellow Power Author Academy cohort. Sometimes I dreaded it, but most times I could not wait to see you those two days every week for the last year. It was an iron sharpens iron experience going through this adventure with you. You are dynamic women with a message the world needs to hear.

Finally, thank YOU for reading *Legally Savvy*! Thank you for investing your time and congratulations for prioritizing this information for yourself. I would love to hear your wins practicing the *Legally Savvy* hacks and highlight your story on a future blog or podcast. Sharing the stories helps us all. If you are interested in having your story shared, please contact me or post on social media using the hashtags #legallysavvy and #belegallysavvy.

Sincerely,
Zarinah

About The Author

Zarinah Nadir is an award-winning American lawyer, educator, social justice advocate, entrepreneur and visionary. Also known as the "legal translator," she has a rare ability to make the law plain and accessible for everyday people. Over this last decade she has been laser-focused on bringing about access to justice to historically disenfranchised individuals, artists, families, communities, emerging entrepreneurs, and seasoned business owners in the United States and Canada to know their rights in areas from civil rights, juvenile law, family law, criminal justice, immigration, and corporate law. Zarinah founded **the Legally Savvy Movement** to disrupt everyday perceptions of lawyers and help people feel more confident, empowered and less stressed while navigating the legalities of love, life, and business. Additionally, she works alongside progressive socially-conscious go-getters to build the largest human rights organizations on the planet bringing affordable access to attorneys to the masses - an essential key to social justice.

Zarinah has served as one the youngest executive leaders both civically in her legislative district, and internationally in pioneering mental health and social justice organizations. For over two decades, she has been a champion for the voiceless. Her longstanding commitment to social justice began at a young age where she played a key role in changing the power balance in her community resulting in more women in leadership. Dubbed a "new traditionalist," her trailblazing life took center stage as the opening story, "Zarinah: An Islamic-style High School Queen," in The Face Behind the Veil: The extraordinary lives of Muslim women by the two Pulitzer Prize participating author Donna Gehrke-White. Committed to diverse representation and her faith, her scholarship has focused on the effects of Islamic religious practices around marriage and inheritance intersecting with U.S. civil law.

Raised in Phoenix to celebrate multiculturalism by woke parents from New York, language is one of her favorite tools for cultural understanding. She graduated with a Bachelor's degree in Spanish from Arizona State University and after the tragic events of September 11th, was inspired to learn law as her next language. Graduating with a Juris Doctor from the Sandra Day O'Connor College of Law at ASU, shortly following her graduation she was appointed as its first African American Muslim woman Director of Admissions. Zarinah is currently adjunct faculty at the University of Dubuque teaching courses in criminal justice and sociology.

She is a highly sought-after speaker and guest on national podcasts. Having contributed to the community since her teens, Zarinah is an Arizona fixture being featured in multiple city of Tempe History Museum exhibits, most recently Tempe's 150 Sesquicentennial Celebration. On a personal note, Zarinah loves being born in Queens but raised in Arizona, loves learning languages, and Zumba!

For more information, private appointments, to book a speaking engagement, or to get lawyered up please reach out through the following methods. Zarinah would love to connect!

 email at zarinah@belegallysavvy.com, or

 @zarinahnadiresq, or

 Zarinah Nadir